Toll House
Heritage Cookbook

Toll House
Heritage Cookbook
A collection of favorite dessert recipes

A RUTLEDGE BOOK

I wish to express my thanks to Alexis Cole Shantz, Manager — Public Relations, for her assistance in coordinating this project; and to Ann N. Dries, Director, Home Economics and Consumer Service, and her staff, Janet Andreas, Jo Ann Billowitz, Wendy Kaye and Lynne M. Paino, for developing and testing all the recipes in this book.

[signature]

Group Product Manager
Baking Products
The Nestlé Company, Inc.

Photography by Gordon E. Smith

Cover art and illustrations by Lauren Rosen

Binder designed by Lori Stein

Many of the photographs in this cookbook were taken at Old Bethpage Village Restoration, a living museum in the county of Nassau, Long Island, New York, that depicts the life and work styles of a rural village in the eighteenth and nineteenth centuries.

Published by Rutledge Books, Inc., 112 Madison Avenue, New York, New York 10016

Library of Congress Catalog Card Number: 80–12851
ISBN: 0–87469–029–3
Printed in the United States of America
First Printing: August, 1980
Second Printing: July, 1981

Contents

Introduction

Our heritage cookbook celebrates the anniversary of something very special.

Fifty years ago, America's favorite cookie, the Toll House Cookie, was created. How that irresistible recipe came about is by now a culinary legend. It took its name from a lovely old toll house on the outskirts of Whitman, Massachusetts. Built in 1709 at the halfway point between Boston and New Bedford, it became a haven where weary travelers stopped for food, drink and rest while they waited for a change of horses.

The historic toll house was purchased by Mr. and Mrs. Wakefield in 1930 and turned into the now-famous Toll House Inn. An excellent cook, Mrs. Wakefield experimented with and improved upon many old dessert recipes. Her incredible baked desserts attracted people from all over New England.

One day she was experimenting with a favorite Colonial cookie recipe, the Butter-Drop Do. She cut a bar of Nestlé Semi-Sweet chocolate into tiny bits and added them to the cookie dough, thinking that they might melt. Instead, the bits of chocolate held their shape, softening just slightly to a delicately creamy texture. Mrs. Wakefield named her delicious discovery the Toll House Cookie.

The Toll House Cookie soon became a widespread favorite. Everybody wanted the recipe to bake at home, so, with Mrs. Wakefield's permission, Nestlé put the recipe right on the wrapper of their semi-sweet chocolate bar.

As the popularity of the Toll House Cookie grew, Nestlé looked for ways to make it easier for people to bake the recipe. They started producing a special chocolate bar that was scored so it could be easily divided into tiny sections. Not long after, Nestlé started offering little pieces of chocolate in convenient ready-to-use packages — and the very first Semi-Sweet Real Chocolate Morsels were introduced to American bakers.

Nestlé Semi-Sweet Morsels have made millions of chocolate lovers happy since they were first created for the original Toll House Cookie. Today they are used to make hundreds of delicious chocolate treats all over America.

Our cookbook is an inspired collection of treats and desserts of all kinds and for every occasion—or for no occasion at all except to satisfy a sweet tooth. Desserts for lunchboxes—and for opulent buffets. Sinfully rich candies. Holiday creations. Cookies kids of all ages dream about. And best of all, most of the recipes are *chocolate:* Nestlé is synonymous with the world's favorite flavor.

Nestlé's Semi-Sweet Real Chocolate Morsels and Milk Chocolate Morsels, and the convenient liquid chocolate flavoring, Choco-bake, are the heart of most of these luscious recipes. In addition, there are plenty of desserts made with another popular flavor, Nestlé's Butterscotch Morsels—and even ultra-rich combinations of the two.

In our heritage cookbook you'll find old-fashioned favorites you've frequently asked for. There are also some new temptations. The versatility of chocolate is deliciously demonstrated, for example, by our breakfast breads—plus a few surprises that illustrate its rich and unusual history.

We invite you to celebrate with us in the best possible way: Come into the kitchen and rediscover the timeless joys of baking and dessert-making.

Cooking with Chocolate

Chocolate "bloom": Chocolate has a high content of cocoa butter. When stored at temperatures that fluctuate from hot to cold, chocolate can develop "bloom"—a grey film caused by the cocoa butter rising to the surface. While this dulls the rich brown chocolate color, it does not affect the taste. When the chocolate melts, it regains its attractive color—don't hesitate to use it.

Storing chocolate: Keep chocolate in a cool, dry place. Storage temperature should be between 60° and 78°F., with relative humidity at less than 50%. Chocolate can be refrigerated, but wrap it tightly so it won't absorb odors. Airtight wrapping will also help prevent moisture from condensing on the chocolate when removed from the refrigerator. Chocolate becomes hard and very brittle when cold, so allow it to come to room temperature before using.

About Nestlé Milk Chocolate Morsels: *Don't* use Nestlé Milk Chocolate Morsels in baked desserts that do not call for *melting* the morsels before blending them in. The milk causes them to become hard when they are baked. You may substitute Nestlé Milk Chocolate Morsels for Nestlé Semi-Sweet Real Chocolate Morsels in recipes such as frostings or sauces that call for melting the morsels. Nestlé Milk Chocolate Morsels can be melted in a dry double boiler or a microwave oven according to the instructions below for melting Nestlé Semi-Sweet Real Chocolate Morsels.

About Nestlé Choco-bake: Convenient liquid Nestlé Choco-bake can be used in any recipe calling for unsweetened chocolate or cocoa powder. It's packaged in handy 1-ounce envelopes. One envelope Nestlé Choco-bake equals 1 square unsweetened baking chocolate or ¼ cup cocoa powder.

About Nestlé Butterscotch Morsels: Melt according to the instructions below for melting Nestlé Semi-Sweet Real Chocolate Morsels.

About Melting Chocolate

Important: The smallest drop of moisture can cause melted chocolate to become lumpy—even a wet spoon, or steam from the double boiler. If this should occur, stir in 1 tablespoon vegetable shortening for every 3 ounces chocolate. Do not use butter as it contains water.

Yield: One 6-ounce package (1 cup) Nestlé Semi-Sweet Real Chocolate Morsels equals ½ cup melted chocolate.

Top of Stove Method: Place Nestlé Semi-Sweet Real Chocolate Morsels in the top of a dry, clean double boiler. Place over hot—not boiling—water. Stir occasionally until smooth.

Microwave Oven Method: *To melt one 6-ounce package (1 cup) Nestlé Semi-Sweet Real Chocolate Morsels:* Place morsels in a dry 2-cup glass measuring cup. Microwave on high 1 minute; stir. Microwave on high 1 minute longer. Stir until chocolate is smooth.

To melt one 12-ounce package (2 cups) Nestlé Semi-Sweet Real Chocolate Morsels: Place morsels in a dry 4-cup glass measuring cup. Microwave on high 2 minutes; stir. Microwave on high 1 minute longer. Stir until chocolate is smooth.

Chocolate Conversion Chart

When recipe calls for:	You may use:
1 oz. (1 square) unsweetened baking chocolate	1 envelope (1 oz.) Nestlé Choco-bake. *Or* 3 oz. (½ cup) Nestlé Semi-Sweet Real Chocolate Morsels; *decrease* shortening (1 T.) and sugar (¼ cup)
3 oz. (3 squares) semi-sweet baking chocolate	3 oz. (½ cup) Nestlé Semi-Sweet Real Chocolate Morsels
¼ cup unsweetened cocoa powder	1 envelope (1 oz.) Nestlé Choco-bake. *Or* 3 oz. (½ cup) Nestlé Semi-Sweet Real Chocolate Morsels; *decrease* shortening (1 T.) and sugar (¼ cup)

Ingredient Substitutions

When recipe calls for:	You may substitute:
1 t. baking powder	¼ t. baking soda + ⅝ t. cream of tartar, *or* ¼ t. baking soda + ½ cup buttermilk or sour milk (to replace ½ cup liquid called for in recipe)
1 cup butter	1 cup margarine *or* 1 cup hydrogenated shortening + ½ t. salt
1 cup buttermilk or sour milk	1 T. vinegar or lemon juice plus enough sweet milk to equal 1 cup (let stand 5 minutes), *or* 1¾ t. cream of tartar + 1 cup sweet milk
1 cup corn syrup	1 cup sugar + ¼ cup liquid*
1 cup heavy cream	⅓ cup butter + about ¾ cup milk
1 cup honey	1¼ cups sugar + ¼ cup liquid*
1 cup brown sugar	1 cup white sugar + ¼ cup molasses
1 cup whole milk	½ cup evaporated milk + ½ cup water, *or* 1 cup reconstituted nonfat dry milk + 2½ t. butter or margarine

Use liquid called for in the particular recipe.

About Unsifted Flour

Our recipes call for "*unsifted* flour." Almost all flours sold today have been *presifted* and should not be sifted again at home before measuring.

About Preheated Ovens

All recipes in this cookbook have been developed, tested and timed using ovens that have been preheated for approximately 10 minutes. With some recipes that have brief baking times, such as cookies, the preheating is critical.

In the Toll House Tradition

Mrs. Wakefield knew what she was doing when she mixed her first batch of Toll House Cookies. Using a time-tested Colonial recipe, she made her dough from just the right amounts of golden brown sugar, farm-fresh eggs and rich creamery butter. Into the finished batter she stirred her own addition—bits of semi-sweet chocolate chopped from a bar of Nestlé's chocolate. The result was the Nestlé Toll House Cookie, a buttery, brown-sugary delight laced with rich spurts of creamy Nestlé Semi-Sweet Chocolate in every bite.

The Nestlé Toll House Cookie went on to become America's favorite cookie. The Semi-Sweet Real Chocolate Morsels produced today are made from the same rich chocolate as the bar that Mrs. Wakefield used. And because we know how much people love the taste of this unique combination of ingredients, we've created a variety of dessert recipes based on the taste and texture of the original Nestlé Toll House Cookie. In this chapter you'll find not only a number of delectable variations of the basic cookie, but some special treats and surprises, too.

Original Toll House® Cookies

2¼   cups *unsifted* flour
1   measuring teaspoon baking soda
1   measuring teaspoon salt
1   cup butter, softened
¾   cup sugar
¾   cup firmly packed brown sugar
1   measuring teaspoon vanilla extract
2   eggs
1   12-ounce package (2 cups) Nestlé Semi-Sweet Real
      Chocolate Morsels
1   cup chopped nuts

Preheat oven to 375°F. In a small bowl, combine flour, baking soda and salt; set aside. In a large bowl, combine butter, sugar, brown sugar and vanilla extract; beat until creamy. Beat in eggs. Gradually add flour mixture; mix well. Stir in Nestlé Semi-Sweet Real Chocolate Morsels and nuts. Drop by rounded teaspoonfuls onto ungreased cookie sheets. Bake 8 to 10 minutes.

Makes 100 2-inch cookies

FLAVOR VARIATIONS: Omit nuts; add one of the following:

4   *cups crisp, ready-to-eat cereal*
2   *cups chopped dates*
2   *cups raisins*
1   *cup peanut butter*
1   *measuring tablespoon grated orange rind*

GIANT TOLL HOUSE COOKIES: Prepare Toll House Cookie dough as directed. Drop dough by ¼ cupfuls onto ungreased cookie sheets; lightly press into 3-inch circles. Bake at 375°F. for 10 to 12 minutes.

Makes about 21 4-inch cookies

VARIATIONS OF ORIGINAL TOLL HOUSE COOKIES

To surprise Toll House Cookie fans with delightful variations on the original recipe, see page 14. As indicated, prepare the dough according to the directions in the original recipe above. The whole wheat variation requires a flour substitution.

Recipe continued on page 14

Original Toll House Cookies

VARIATIONS OF ORIGINAL TOLL HOUSE COOKIES

PAN COOKIE VARIATION: Prepare Toll House Cookie dough as directed. Spread into greased 15x10x1-inch baking pan. Bake at 375°F. for 20 minutes. Cool; cut into thirty-five 2-inch squares.

Note: Recipe may be divided in half (use a 6-ounce package of Nestlé Semi-Sweet Real Chocolate Morsels; halve the amounts of all other ingredients). Spread dough into greased 9-inch square baking pan. Bake at 375°F. for 20 to 25 minutes. Cool; cut into about sixteen 2-inch squares. For a crisper pan cookie, spread dough into greased 13x9x2-inch baking pan. Bake at 375°F. for 12 to 15 minutes. Cool; cut into twenty-four 2-inch squares.

WHOLE WHEAT TOLL HOUSE COOKIES: Substitute unsifted whole wheat flour for either the total amount of flour (2¼ cups) or substitute unsifted whole wheat flour for half the amount of flour (use 1 cup + 2 measuring tablespoons each whole wheat and all purpose flour). Note: Cookies made with whole wheat flour are darker than traditional Toll House Cookies.

Holiday dessert ideas: The Quick Party Log on page 133 is our delicious and easy version of the traditional Bûche de Nöel, or Yule Log. Throughout the book are a number of desserts that are perfect for holiday meals or celebrations; many are illustrated. Some suggestions:

Valentine's Day: Pink Peppermint Pie, Valentine Ice Cream Torte
Washington's Birthday: Black Forest Cherry Torte
St. Patrick's Day: Chocolate-Mint Soufflé, Grasshopper Pie
Easter: Bird's Nest Coffeecake
Fourth of July: Black Forest Cherry Torte; coolers such as Blender Chocolate Ice Cream and Old-Fashioned Mocha Shake
Halloween: Apple Cartwheels, Halloween Squares
Thanksgiving: Butterscotch-Apple Crisp, Indian Pudding, Pumpkin Chiffon Pie
Christmas: Butterscotch People, Chocolate-Raspberry Trifle, Holiday Steamed Pudding, Miniature Chocolate Fruitcakes, Sherry Fruitcake, Quick Party Log
New Year's Eve: Chocolate Fruit Soup, Easy Chocolate Fondue

Refrigerator Toll House Cookies

2¼   **cups *unsifted* flour**
  1   **measuring teaspoon baking soda**
  1   **measuring teaspoon salt**
  1   **cup butter, softened**
¾   **cup sugar**
¾   **cup firmly packed brown sugar**
  1   **measuring teaspoon vanilla extract**
  2   **eggs**
  1   **12-ounce package (2 cups) Nestlé Semi-Sweet Real**
         Chocolate Morsels
  1   **cup chopped nuts**

In a small bowl, combine flour, baking soda and salt; set aside. In a large bowl, combine butter, sugar, brown sugar and vanilla extract; beat until creamy. Beat in eggs. Gradually add flour mixture; mix well. Stir in Nestlé Semi-Sweet Real Chocolate Morsels and nuts. Divide dough in half; wrap both halves separately in waxed paper. Chill 1 hour, or until firm. On waxed paper, shape each dough half into a 12-inch log. Roll up in waxed paper; refrigerate up to 1 week or freeze up to 8 weeks.

To bake, preheat oven to 375°F. Cut each chilled log into twelve 1-inch slices. Cut each slice into 4 quarters. Place on ungreased cookie sheets. Bake 8 to 10 minutes.

Makes 8 dozen cookies

Like money in the bank! Refrigerator Toll House Cookies are one way to make sure the cookie jar is always filled with everybody's favorite. Store a few "logs" in the freezer—then you'll be able to have fresh-baked cookies at a moment's notice.

Pizza Cookie

COOKIE

2¼	**cups _unsifted_ flour**
1	**measuring teaspoon baking soda**
1	**measuring teaspoon salt**
1	**cup butter, softened**
¾	**cup sugar**
¾	**cup firmly packed brown sugar**
1	**measuring teaspoon vanilla extract**
2	**eggs**
1	**12-ounce package (2 cups) Nestlé Semi-Sweet Real Chocolate Morsels**
1	**cup chopped nuts**

FROSTING

1	**6-ounce package (1 cup) Nestlé Semi-Sweet Real Chocolate Morsels**
1	**6-ounce package (1 cup) Nestlé Butterscotch Morsels**

Preheat oven to 375°F. In a small bowl, combine flour, baking soda and salt; set aside. In a large bowl, combine butter, sugar, brown sugar and vanilla extract; beat until creamy. Beat in eggs. Gradually add flour mixture; mix well. Stir in Nestlé Semi-Sweet Real Chocolate Morsels and nuts. Spread into greased 14-inch round pizza pan. Bake 25 minutes. Remove from oven. Sprinkle half of top with Nestlé Semi-Sweet Real Chocolate Morsels and other half with Nestlé Butterscotch Morsels. Let set for 5 minutes to soften morsels. To frost, spread softened morsels evenly over cookie. Cool completely. Cut into wedges.

Makes one 14-inch round cookie

Cookie Brittle

1 **cup butter, softened**
1 **cup sugar**
1½ **measuring teaspoons vanilla extract**
1 **measuring teaspoon salt**
2 **cups *unsifted* flour**
1 **6-ounce package (1 cup) Nestlé Semi-Sweet Real Chocolate Morsels**
½ **cup chopped nuts**

Preheat oven to 375°F. In a large bowl, combine butter, sugar, vanilla extract and salt; beat until creamy. Gradually blend in flour. Stir in Nestlé Semi-Sweet Real Chocolate Morsels. Press evenly into ungreased 15x10x1-inch baking pan. Sprinkle nuts over top. Bake 25 minutes. Cool; break into irregular pieces.

Makes about 1¾ pounds brittle

Double Chocolate Brownies

¾ **cup *unsifted* flour**
¼ **measuring teaspoon baking soda**
¼ **measuring teaspoon salt**
⅓ **cup butter**
¾ **cup sugar**
2 **measuring tablespoons water**
1 **12-ounce package (2 cups) Nestlé Semi-Sweet Real Chocolate Morsels, divided**
1 **measuring teaspoon vanilla extract**
2 **eggs**
½ **cup chopped nuts**

Preheat oven to 325°F. In a small bowl, combine flour, baking soda and salt; set aside. In a small saucepan, combine butter, sugar and water. Bring *just to a boil,* then remove from heat. Add 6-ounces (1 cup) Nestlé Semi-Sweet Real Chocolate Morsels and vanilla extract. Stir until morsels melt and mixture is smooth. Transfer to a large bowl. Add eggs, one at a time, beating well after each addition. Gradually blend in flour mixture. Stir in remaining 1 cup Nestlé Semi-Sweet Real Chocolate Morsels and the nuts. Spread into greased 9-inch square baking pan. Bake 30 to 35 minutes. Cool completely. Cut into 2¼-inch squares.

Makes 16 2¼-inch squares

Golden Brownies

2¼ cups *unsifted* flour
2½ measuring teaspoons baking powder
 ½ measuring teaspoon salt
 ¾ cup butter, softened
1¼ cups sugar
1¼ cups firmly packed light brown sugar
  1 measuring teaspoon vanilla extract
  3 eggs
  1 12-ounce package (2 cups) Nestlé Semi-Sweet Real
     Chocolate Morsels

Preheat oven to 350°F. In a small bowl, combine flour, baking powder and salt; set aside. In a large bowl, beat butter, sugar, brown sugar and vanilla extract until creamy. Add eggs, one at a time, beating well after each addition. Gradually beat in flour mixture. Stir in Nestlé Semi-Sweet Real Chocolate Morsels. Spread evenly into well-greased 15x10x1-inch baking pan. Bake 35 to 40 minutes. Cool; cut into 2-inch squares.

Makes 35 2-inch squares

Oatmeal Marble Squares

 ¾ cup *unsifted* flour
 ½ measuring teaspoon baking soda
 ½ measuring teaspoon salt
 ½ cup butter, softened
  6 measuring tablespoons sugar
  6 measuring tablespoons firmly packed brown sugar
 ½ measuring teaspoon vanilla extract
  1 egg
  1 cup uncooked quick oats
 ½ cup chopped nuts
  1 6-ounce package (1 cup) Nestlé Semi-Sweet Real
     Chocolate Morsels

Preheat oven to 375°F. In a small bowl, combine flour, baking soda and salt; set aside. In a large bowl, combine butter, sugar, brown sugar and vanilla extract; beat until creamy. Beat in egg. Blend in flour mixture. Stir in oats and nuts. Spread into greased 13x9x2-inch baking pan. Sprinkle Nestlé Semi-Sweet Real Chocolate Morsels over top. Place in oven for 3 minutes. Run knife through to marbleize. Bake 10 to 12 minutes. Cool; cut into 2-inch squares.

Makes 2 dozen 2-inch squares

Golden Peanut Butter Brownies

2¼   cups *unsifted* flour
2½   measuring teaspoons baking powder
 ½   measuring teaspoon salt
 ⅔   cup butter, softened
 ⅔   cup creamy peanut butter
1¼   cups sugar
1¼   cups firmly packed brown sugar
  1   measuring teaspoon vanilla extract
  3   eggs
  1   6-ounce package (1 cup) Nestlé Semi-Sweet Real
        Chocolate Morsels

Preheat oven to 350°F. In a small bowl, combine flour, baking powder and salt; set aside. In a large bowl, combine butter, peanut butter, sugar, brown sugar and vanilla extract; beat until creamy. Add eggs, one at a time, beating well after each addition. Gradually beat in flour mixture. Stir in Nestlé Semi-Sweet Real Chocolate Morsels. Spread evenly into well-greased 15x10x1-inch baking pan. Bake 35 minutes. Remove from oven.* Cool completely. Cut into 2-inch squares.

Makes 35 2-inch squares

* If a frosting is desired, sprinkle top with one 6-ounce package (1 cup) Nestlé Semi-Sweet Real Chocolate Morsels immediately after removing from oven. Let stand about 5 minutes until morsels become shiny and soft; then spread chocolate evenly over top of brownies.

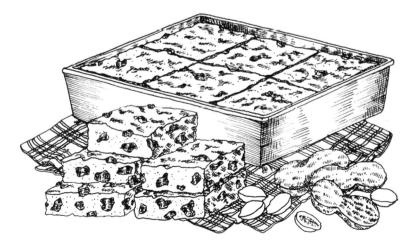

*Golden Brownies, Golden Cupcakes,
Golden Deluxe Cake*

Golden Deluxe Cake

CAKE

3 cups *unsifted* flour
1 measuring tablespoon baking powder
1 measuring teaspoon salt
1 cup butter, softened
2 cups firmly packed brown sugar
1 measuring tablespoon vanilla extract
4 eggs
1 cup milk
1 12-ounce package (2 cups) Nestlé Semi-Sweet Real Chocolate Morsels, divided

CHOCOLATE GLAZE

½ cup (3 ounces) Nestlé Semi-Sweet Real Chocolate Morsels, reserved from 12-ounce package
¼ cup boiling water
1 cup sifted confectioners' sugar

CAKE: Preheat oven to 350°F. In a small bowl, combine flour, baking powder and salt; set aside. In a large bowl, combine butter, brown sugar and vanilla extract; beat until creamy. Add eggs, one at a time, beating well after each addition. Blend in flour mixture alternately with milk. Stir in 1½ cups Nestlé Semi-Sweet Real Chocolate Morsels. Spoon batter evenly into well-greased and floured 10-inch fluted or plain tube pan. Bake 1 hour. Cool 15 minutes; remove from pan and cool completely. Pour Chocolate Glaze (below) over top of cake. Let glaze set at room temperature 15 minutes before serving.

CHOCOLATE GLAZE: In blender container, combine remaining ½ cup Nestlé Semi-Sweet Real Chocolate Morsels and boiling water; process at high speed until smooth. Gradually blend in confectioners' sugar; process until smooth. Refrigerate 20 minutes or until desired consistency.

Makes one 10-inch ring cake and ¾ cup glaze

GOLDEN DELUXE LOAF CAKES: Preheat oven to 325°F. Prepare batter as directed above; spoon into two well-greased and floured 9x5x3-inch loaf pans. Bake 60 to 65 minutes. Proceed as directed.

Makes 2 loaf cakes

Golden Cupcakes

CUPCAKES

1 cup plus 2 measuring tablespoons *unsifted* flour
½ measuring teaspoon baking soda
½ measuring teaspoon salt
½ cup butter, softened
6 measuring tablespoons sugar
6 measuring tablespoons firmly packed brown sugar
½ measuring teaspoon vanilla extract
1 egg

TOPPING

½ cup firmly packed brown sugar
1 egg
⅛ measuring teaspoon salt
1 6-ounce package (1 cup) Nestlé Semi-Sweet Real
   Chocolate Morsels
½ cup chopped nuts
½ measuring teaspoon vanilla extract

CUPCAKES: Preheat oven to 375°F. In a small bowl, combine flour, baking soda and salt; set aside. In a large bowl, combine butter, sugar, brown sugar and vanilla extract; beat until creamy. Beat in egg. Blend in flour mixture. Spoon mixture into 16 paper-lined muffin cups, using 1 rounded measuring tablespoon batter for each. Bake 15 minutes. Remove from oven. Increase oven temperature to 425°F. Spoon 1 measuring tablespoon topping (below) over each cupcake. Return to oven. Bake 8 to 10 minutes longer. Cool completely before removing from muffin cups.

TOPPING: In a small bowl, combine brown sugar, egg and salt; beat at high speed until thick (about 5 minutes). Stir in Nestlé Semi-Sweet Real Chocolate Morsels, nuts and vanilla extract.

Makes 16 cupcakes

Instant decorations: Nestlé Morsels—Semi-Sweet Real Chocolate, Milk Chocolate and Butterscotch—can be used in dozens of ways to decorate pies and cakes. Good for last-minute dress-ups, too. Combine for colorful effect, or use alone. Border a pie; top off dollops of frosting or whipped cream; arrange mosaic designs and patterns.

Rich Crumb Cake

CAKE

- **3 cups *unsifted* flour**
- **1 measuring tablespoon baking powder**
- **1 measuring teaspoon baking soda**
- **1 measuring teaspoon salt**
- **1 cup butter, softened**
- **½ cup sugar**
- **½ cup firmly packed brown sugar**
- **3 eggs**
- **1 cup sour cream**
- **1 12-ounce package (2 cups) Nestlé Semi-Sweet Real Chocolate Morsels, divided**

TOPPING

- **1 cup *unsifted* flour**
- **¼ cup firmly packed brown sugar**
- **¼ measuring teaspoon salt**
- **½ cup butter, softened**

CAKE: Preheat oven to 350°F. In a small bowl, combine flour, baking powder, baking soda and salt; set aside. In a large bowl, combine butter, sugar and brown sugar; beat until creamy. Add eggs, one at a time, beating well after each addition. Add flour mixture alternately with sour cream. Stir in 1 cup Nestlé Semi-Sweet Real Chocolate Morsels. Spread into well-greased 13x9x2-inch baking pan. Sprinkle with topping (below). Bake 40 to 45 minutes.

TOPPING: In a small bowl, combine flour, brown sugar and salt. Using a pastry blender or two knives, cut in butter until mixture resembles coarse crumbs. Add remaining 1 cup Nestlé Semi-Sweet Real Chocolate Morsels; mix well.

Makes one 13x9x2-inch crumb cake

Toll House Walnut Pie

2 eggs
½ cup *unsifted* flour
½ cup sugar
½ cup firmly packed brown sugar
1 cup butter, melted and cooled to room temperature
1 6-ounce package (1 cup) Nestlé Semi-Sweet Real
  Chocolate Morsels
1 cup chopped walnuts
1 9-inch unbaked pie shell
  Whipped cream or ice cream (optional)

Preheat oven to 325°F. In a large bowl, beat eggs until foamy; beat in flour, sugar and brown sugar until well blended. Blend in melted butter. Stir in Nestlé Semi-Sweet Real Chocolate Morsels and walnuts. Pour into pie shell. Bake 1 hour. Serve warm with whipped cream or ice cream, if desired.

Makes one 9-inch pie

Golden Meringue Frosting

2 egg whites*
1 cup firmly packed brown sugar
1 measuring teaspoon vanilla extract
1 6-ounce package (1 cup) Nestlé Semi-Sweet Real
  Chocolate Morsels

Preheat oven to 400°F. In a small bowl, beat egg whites until foamy. Gradually add brown sugar and vanilla extract, beating until stiff peaks form. Stir in Nestlé Semi-Sweet Real Chocolate Morsels. Spread on a baked 13x9x2-inch cake (chocolate, spice or your favorite flavor). Bake 8 to 10 minutes.

Makes 2⅔ cups frosting

* Save the yolks for scrambled eggs!

Toll House Walnut Pie

Candies and Confections

Do you remember the delicious Christmas bustle, and how you helped prepare the sweets that welcomed guests and served as loving gifts to family and close friends? The fudge you made on a rainy afternoon that Dad said was the best he ever tasted? And later, the sleep-over where you and your friends trooped into the kitchen to make candy at one in the morning?

These are joyous traditions to continue, pleasures that remain unchanged by the years or fashion. That warmth of yesterday can be captured by the meltingly rich chocolate and butterscotch recipes in this chapter. It is a collection of treats that your whole family will enjoy.

Just one bite of this old-fashioned goodness and the happy memories will come flooding back. And for the youngsters, these new pleasures will become tomorrow's best memories, all to pass on, generation to generation.

Mocha-Rum Truffles

1 **12-ounce package (2 cups) Nestlé Semi-Sweet Real Chocolate Morsels**
½ **cup butter, softened**
4 **egg yolks**
2 **measuring tablespoons rum**
2 **measuring teaspoons instant coffee**
   Confectioners' sugar
   Candied fruit and/or Nestlé Milk Chocolate Morsels and/or Nestlé Butterscotch Morsels (all optional)

Melt Nestlé Semi-Sweet Real Chocolate Morsels over hot (not boiling) water; remove from heat but keep chocolate over hot water. Add butter and egg yolks; beat with wire whisk or fork until smooth. In a small bowl, combine rum and coffee. Add chocolate mixture; stir until smooth. Set bowl over an ice bath; chill mixture 20 to 25 minutes, stirring occasionally, until fudge-like in consistency (yet smooth and creamy). Mixture will be quite thick. Fill a pastry bag fitted with rosette tip with a third of the chocolate mixture. Pipe 1-inch rosettes onto cookie sheets.* Sift confectioners' sugar over candies. Decorate with candied fruit and/or Nestlé Milk Chocolate Morsels and/or Nestlé Butterscotch Morsels, if desired. Repeat with remaining chocolate mixture. Let candies stand at room temperature several hours to season.

Makes 5 dozen 1-inch candies

* Chocolate mixture may be shaped into 1-inch balls, then rolled in confectioners' sugar.

Two-Tone Bites

1   **12-ounce package (2 cups) Nestlé Butterscotch Morsels**
1   **measuring tablespoon butter**
1   **measuring tablespoon water**
1   **cup chopped nuts**
1   **6-ounce package (1 cup) Nestlé Semi-Sweet Real Chocolate Morsels**
3   **measuring tablespoons corn syrup**
1   **measuring tablespoon water**

Over hot (not boiling) water, combine Nestlé Butterscotch Morsels, butter and water. Stir until morsels melt and mixture is smooth. Add nuts; mix well. Press into foil-lined 8-inch square pan. Over hot (not boiling) water, combine Nestlé Semi-Sweet Real Chocolate Morsels, corn syrup and water; stir until morsels melt and mixture is smooth. Pour chocolate mixture evenly over butterscotch layer. Chill until firm (about 2 hours). Cut into 1-inch squares.

Makes 64 1-inch candies

Snow Caps

1   **12-ounce package (2 cups) Nestlé Semi-Sweet Real Chocolate Morsels**
¼   **cup dark corn syrup**
1   **measuring tablespoon water**
1   **cup chopped nuts**
    Sugar
1   **8-ounce package cream cheese, softened**
⅔   **cup sifted confectioners' sugar**
2   **measuring teaspoons vanilla extract**
    Walnut pieces (optional)

Over hot (not boiling) water, combine Nestlé Semi-Sweet Real Chocolate Morsels, corn syrup and water; heat until morsels melt and mixture is smooth. Stir in chopped nuts. Drop by slightly rounded measuring teaspoonfuls onto waxed paper lined cookie sheets; press flat with bottom of glass dipped in sugar. Chill in refrigerator for 5 minutes. In a small bowl, combine cream cheese, confectioners' sugar and vanilla extract; beat until creamy. Top each chocolate mound with 1 measuring teaspoonful of cream cheese frosting. Garnish with walnut pieces, if desired. Return to refrigerator and chill until firm. Store in airtight container in refrigerator.

Makes 3½ dozen 1½-inch candies

From top: Two-Tone Bites,
Mocha-Rum Truffles, Snow Caps,
Chocolate-Mint Fancies

Chocolate-Mint Fancies

CHOCOLATE LAYERS

1 12-ounce package (2 cups) Nestlé Semi-Sweet Real Chocolate Morsels, divided
4 measuring tablespoons vegetable shortening, divided

FONDANT FILLING

5 measuring tablespoons butter
½ cup light corn syrup
4½ cups sifted confectioners' sugar, divided
1 measuring teaspoon peppermint extract
Red or green food coloring

CHOCOLATE BOTTOM LAYER: Over hot (not boiling) water, combine 1 cup Nestlé Semi-Sweet Real Chocolate Morsels and 2 measuring tablespoons shortening; heat until morsels melt and mixture is smooth. Spread evenly with back of spoon in foil-lined 15x10x1-inch pan. Chill in refrigerator until firm (about 20 minutes). Carefully invert onto waxed paper lined cookie sheet. Gently peel off foil. Return to refrigerator.

FONDANT FILLING: In a large saucepan, combine butter, corn syrup, and half the confectioners' sugar; bring to *full boil,* stirring constantly over *medium-low* heat. Add remaining confectioners' sugar, the peppermint extract and desired amount of food coloring; stir vigorously until well blended (about 3 minutes). Remove from heat. Pour fondant onto greased cookie sheet. Cool long enough to handle (about 5 minutes). Knead until soft (about 2 to 3 minutes). Roll out fondant ⅛ inch thick between two pieces of plastic wrap to form a 15x10-inch rectangle. Remove top sheet of plastic wrap. Carefully invert fondant onto chocolate bottom layer. Remove second sheet of plastic wrap. Chill 15 minutes.

CHOCOLATE TOP LAYER: Over hot (not boiling) water, combine remaining 1 cup Nestlé Semi-Sweet Real Chocolate Morsels and 2 measuring tablespoons vegetable shortening; heat until morsels melt and mixture is smooth. Spread evenly over fondant filling. Chill 15 to 20 minutes.

Cut out 24 shapes with a 2-inch cookie cutter. Chill in refrigerator until ready to serve.

Makes 2 dozen 2-inch candies

Butterscotch Fudge Ring

1   **6-ounce package (1 cup) Nestlé Semi-Sweet Real Chocolate Morsels**
1   **6-ounce package (1 cup) Nestlé Butterscotch Morsels**
1   **14-ounce can sweetened condensed milk**
1   **cup coarsely chopped walnuts**
½   **measuring teaspoon vanilla extract**
1   **cup walnut halves, divided**
   Maraschino cherry halves (optional)

Over hot (not boiling) water, combine Nestlé Semi-Sweet Real Chocolate Morsels, Nestlé Butterscotch Morsels and sweetened condensed milk; heat until morsels melt and mixture is smooth and slightly thickened. Remove from heat; stir in chopped walnuts and vanilla extract. Chill in refrigerator until mixture thickens (about 1 hour). Line bottom of 9-inch pie pan with a 12-inch square piece of foil. On the foil, arrange ¾ cup of the walnut halves in a 2-inch-wide flat ring. Spoon small mounds of chocolate-butterscotch mixture on top of walnuts to form a ring. Decorate with remaining ¼ cup walnut halves and, if desired, maraschino cherries. Chill in refrigerator until firm enough to slice (about 1 hour). Cut into ½-inch slices.

Makes 3 dozen candies

Deluxe Fudge

2   cups sugar
¾   cup evaporated milk
2   measuring tablespoons butter
½   measuring teaspoon salt
1   5-ounce Nestlé King-Size Milk Chocolate Bar, broken into small pieces
2   envelopes (2-ounces) Nestlé Choco-bake
1   measuring teaspoon vanilla extract

In a small saucepan, combine sugar, evaporated milk, butter and salt. Bring to *full boil* over moderate heat, stirring occasionally. *Boil 5 minutes* over moderate heat, stirring constantly. Remove from heat. Add Nestlé Milk Chocolate Bar, Nestlé Choco-bake and vanilla extract; stir until chocolate melts and mixture is smooth. Pour into foil-lined 8-inch square pan. Chill in refrigerator until firm (about 2 hours). Cut into 1-inch squares.

Makes 1½ pounds candy

Easy Peanut Butter Fudge

1   6-ounce package (1 cup) Nestlé Semi-Sweet Real Chocolate Morsels
1   6-ounce package (1 cup) Nestlé Butterscotch Morsels
1   cup chunky peanut butter
1   14-ounce can sweetened condensed milk,* divided
2   cups oven-toasted rice cereal
1   cup miniature marshmallows

Over hot (not boiling) water, melt Nestlé Semi-Sweet Real Chocolate Morsels and Nestlé Butterscotch Morsels; set aside. In a large bowl, blend together peanut butter and ¼ cup of the sweetened condensed milk. Stir in cereal. Reserve ½ cup peanut butter mixture and spread remainder into greased 9-inch square pan. Sprinkle miniature marshmallows on top. Combine remaining sweetened condensed milk with chocolate-butterscotch mixture. Spread evenly over marshmallows. Sprinkle reserved peanut butter mixture on top and press in lightly. Chill in refrigerator until firm (at least 2 hours). Cut into 2¼x1-inch bars.

Makes 3 dozen 2¼x1-inch candies

* Not evaporated milk

Marshmallow Cream Fudge

1   jar marshmallow cream (5 to 10 ounces)
1½ cups sugar
⅔   cup evaporated milk
¼   cup butter
¼   measuring teaspoon salt
1   12-ounce package (2 cups) Nestlé Semi-Sweet Real
      Chocolate Morsels
½   cup chopped nuts
1   measuring teaspoon vanilla extract

In a medium saucepan, combine marshmallow cream, sugar, evaporated milk, butter and salt; bring to *full boil,* stirring constantly over moderate heat. *Boil 5 minutes,* stirring constantly over moderate heat. Remove from heat. Add Nestlé Semi-Sweet Real Chocolate Morsels; stir until morsels melt and mixture is smooth. Stir in nuts and vanilla extract. Pour into foil-lined 8-inch square pan. Chill in refrigerator until firm (about 2 hours).

Makes 2¼ pounds candy

Bourbon Balls

1   6-ounce package (1 cup) Nestlé Semi-Sweet Real
      Chocolate Morsels
3   measuring tablespoons corn syrup
½   cup bourbon
2½ cups vanilla wafer crumbs
½   cup sifted confectioners' sugar
1   cup finely chopped nuts
      Granulated sugar

Over hot (not boiling) water, melt Nestlé Semi-Sweet Real Chocolate Morsels; remove from heat. Blend in corn syrup and bourbon. In a large bowl, combine vanilla wafer crumbs, confectioners' sugar and nuts. Add chocolate mixture; mix well. Let stand about 30 minutes. Form into 1-inch balls. Roll in granulated sugar. Let season in a covered container for several days.

Makes 4½ dozen 1-inch candies

From top: Mix 'Ems, Bourbon Balls,
Marshmallow Cream Fudge

Creamy Chocolate Fudge

1	jar marshmallow cream (5 to 10 ounces)
1½	cups sugar
⅔	cup evaporated milk
¼	cup butter
¼	measuring teaspoon salt
1	11½-ounce package (2 cups) Nestlé Milk Chocolate Morsels
1	6-ounce package (1 cup) Nestlé Semi-Sweet Real Chocolate Morsels
½	cup chopped nuts
1	measuring teaspoon vanilla extract

In a large saucepan, combine marshmallow cream, sugar, evaporated milk, butter and salt; bring to *full boil* over moderate heat, stirring constantly. *Boil 5 minutes* over moderate heat, stirring constantly. Remove from heat. Add Nestlé Milk Chocolate Morsels and Nestlé Semi-Sweet Real Chocolate Morsels; stir until morsels melt and mixture is well blended. Stir in nuts and vanilla extract. Pour into foil-lined 8-inch square pan. Chill in refrigerator until firm (about 2 hours).

Makes 2½ pounds candy

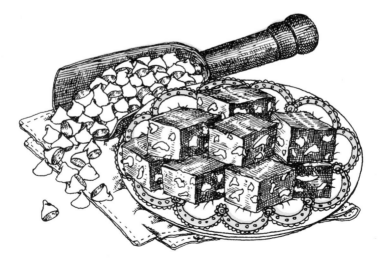

Chocolate-Almond Bark

1　11½-ounce package (2 cups) Nestlé Milk Chocolate
　　Morsels
1　measuring tablespoon vegetable shortening
½　cup whole almonds
½　cup raisins

Line a 13x9x2-inch baking pan with a sheet of waxed paper about
16 inches long (so that candy can be easily lifted out of the pan).
Over hot (not boiling) water, combine Nestlé Milk Chocolate
Morsels and shortening; heat until morsels melt and mixture is
smooth. Remove from heat and stir in almonds and raisins. Spread
into waxed paper lined pan. Chill in refrigerator about 15 minutes;
remove and score top with tines of fork to resemble bark. Return to
refrigerator and chill until ready to serve, at least 30 minutes. Before
serving, break into bite-size pieces.

Makes 1 pound candy

Crispy Fudge Sandwiches

1　6-ounce package (1 cup) Nestlé Butterscotch Morsels
½　cup chunky peanut butter
4　cups oven-toasted rice cereal
1　6-ounce package (1 cup) Nestlé Semi-Sweet Real
　　Chocolate Morsels
½　cup sifted confectioners' sugar
2　measuring tablespoons butter
1　measuring tablespoon water

In a large saucepan, combine Nestlé Butterscotch Morsels and peanut butter; heat until morsels melt and mixture is smooth. Add cereal; stir until well coated. Press half the butterscotch mixture into
buttered 8-inch square pan. Chill in refrigerator while preparing
fudge mixture. Set aside remaining butterscotch mixture. Over hot
(not boiling) water, combine Nestlé Semi-Sweet Real Chocolate
Morsels, confectioners' sugar, butter and water; stir until morsels
melt and mixture is smooth. Spread over chilled butterscotch mixture. Spread remaining butterscotch mixture evenly over top. Press
gently. Chill until firm (about 1 hour). Cut into 1½- inch squares.
Makes 25　1½-inch candies

Turtles

1   **pound (56) vanilla caramels**
¼   **cup butter**
2   **measuring tablespoons water**
1   **11½-ounce package (2 cups) Nestlé Milk Chocolate Morsels***
½   **cup light corn syrup**
2   **measuring tablespoons water**
    Pecan halves (about 2 cups)

Over boiling water, combine caramels, butter and 2 measuring tablespoons water; heat until caramels melt and mixture is smooth. Keep warm over boiling water. Over hot (not boiling) water, combine Nestlé Milk Chocolate Morsels, corn syrup and 2 measuring tablespoons water; heat until morsels melt and mixture is smooth. Keep warm over hot water. Drop caramel mixture by ½ measuring teaspoonfuls onto greased cookie sheets. Arrange 3 pecan halves on top of each caramel to make turtle head and legs. Drop chocolate mixture over caramel-nut piece by slightly rounded measuring teaspoonful. Chill in refrigerator until set (about 20 minutes). Remove from refrigerator and allow to soften slightly before serving.

Makes about 4 dozen candies

*One 12-ounce package (2 cups) Nestlé Semi-Sweet Real Chocolate Morsels may be substituted for Nestlé Milk Chocolate Morsels.

Fudge Drops

1   **6-ounce package (1 cup) Nestlé Semi-Sweet Real Chocolate Morsels**
1   **6-ounce package (1 cup) Nestlé Butterscotch Morsels**
1¼ **cups natural cereal**
1   **cup chopped cashews**
    Whole walnuts, pecans or cashews (optional)

Over hot (not boiling) water, combine Nestlé Semi-Sweet Real Chocolate Morsels and Nestlé Butterscotch Morsels; stir until morsels melt and mixture is smooth. Remove from heat; stir in cereal and chopped cashews. Drop by rounded measuring teaspoonfuls onto waxed paper lined cookie sheets. Garnish with whole nuts, if desired. Chill in refrigerator until firm (about 30 minutes).

Makes about 4 dozen candies

Left, from top: Banana Pops,
Halloween Squares, Chocolate-Covered Pretzels.
Right: Turtles

Hopscotchers

 1   **12 -ounce package (2 cups) Nestlé Butterscotch Morsels**
 ½   **cup light corn syrup**
 2   **measuring tablespoons water**
 1   **measuring tablespoon vegetable shortening**
 2   **3-ounce cans chow mein noodles**
 4   **cups miniature marshmallows or 1 8-ounce package chopped dates**

Over hot (not boiling) water, combine Nestlé Butterscotch Morsels, corn syrup, water and shortening; heat until morsels melt and mixture is smooth. Transfer to a large bowl. Add noodles; mix well. Cool slightly; fold in marshmallows or dates. Drop by slightly rounded measuring tablespoonfuls onto waxed paper lined cookie sheets. Chill in refrigerator until firm (about 20 minutes).

Makes 4 dozen candies

PEANUT BUTTER HOPSCOTCHERS: Substitute 1 cup peanut butter for the corn syrup and water.

Chocolate-Covered Pretzels

 1   **6-ounce package (1 cup) Nestlé Semi-Sweet Real Chocolate Morsels**
 2   **measuring tablespoons corn syrup**
 2   **measuring tablespoons vegetable shortening**
 1½   **measuring teaspoons water**
     3-inch twisted pretzels (25 to 30)

Over hot (not boiling) water, combine Nestlé Semi-Sweet Real Chocolate Morsels, corn syrup, shortening and water; stir until morsels melt and mixture is smooth. Remove from heat but keep mixture over hot water. Dip pretzels into chocolate mixture to coat evenly. Place pretzels on wire racks set over waxed paper. Chill in refrigerator until coating sets (about 10 minutes). Remove from refrigerator and let stand at room temperature until surface dries (about 1 hour).

Makes 25 to 30 pretzels

Mix 'Ems

Mix together in a plastic bag or container one (or more) of the following combinations:

1   **6-ounce package (1 cup) Nestlé Semi-Sweet Real Chocolate or Nestlé Butterscotch Morsels**
1   **cup salted peanuts**
1   **cup raisins**

1   **6-ounce package (1 cup) Nestlé Semi-Sweet Real Chocolate or Nestlé Butterscotch Morsels**
1   **cup potato sticks**
1   **cup coarsely broken pretzel sticks**

1   **6-ounce package (1 cup) Nestlé Semi-Sweet Real Chocolate or Nestlé Butterscotch Morsels**
1   **cup coarsely broken peanut brittle**
1   **cup raisins**

1   **6-ounce package (1 cup) Nestlé Semi-Sweet Real Chocolate Morsels**
1   **6-ounce package (1 cup) Nestlé Butterscotch Morsels**
1   **cup broken corn chips**

1   **6-ounce package (1 cup) Nestlé Semi-Sweet Real Chocolate or Nestlé Butterscotch Morsels**
1   **cup ready-to-eat cereal**
1   **cup raisins**

1   **6-ounce package (1 cup) Nestlé Semi-Sweet Real Chocolate or Nestlé Butterscotch Morsels**
1   **8-ounce package (1½ cups) chopped dates**
1   **cup salted cashews**

1   **6-ounce package (1 cup) Nestlé Semi-Sweet Real Chocolate or Nestlé Butterscotch Morsels**

Chocolate-Dipped Fruit

Chocolate-Dipped Fruit

1   **12-ounce package (2 cups) Nestlé Semi-Sweet Real Chocolate Morsels**
¼   **cup vegetable shortening**
      Fresh strawberries, washed and dried, or
      Mandarin orange slices, drained, or
      Pineapple chunks, drained, or
      Maraschino cherries, drained

Over hot (not boiling) water, combine Nestlé Semi-Sweet Real Chocolate Morsels and shortening; stir until morsels melt and mixture is smooth. Remove from heat but keep chocolate over hot water.* (If chocolate begins to set, return to heat. Add 1 to 2 measuring teaspoons shortening; stir until smooth.) Dip pieces of desired fruit into chocolate mixture, shaking off excess chocolate. Place on foil-lined cookie sheets. Chill in refrigerator 10 to 15 minutes until chocolate is set. Gently loosen fruit from foil with metal spatula. Chocolate-Dipped Fruit may be kept at room temperature up to 1 hour. If chocolate becomes sticky, return to refrigerator.

Makes 1 cup melted chocolate

* *To make in electric fondue pot or skillet, set at low:* Combine Nestlé Semi-Sweet Real Chocolate Morsels and shortening. Stir until morsels melt and mixture is smooth. Keep heat set at low. Proceed as directed.

Chocolate Coating

1   **6-ounce package (1 cup) Nestlé Semi-Sweet Real Chocolate Morsels**
2   **measuring tablespoons vegetable shortening**

Over hot (not boiling) water, combine Nestlé Semi-Sweet Real Chocolate Morsels and shortening; heat until morsels melt and mixture is smooth. Remove from heat but keep mixture over hot water. Dip candy, cookies or pretzels into chocolate mixture to coat evenly. Place on wire racks set over waxed paper. Coating will set in about 10 minutes at room temperature.

Makes ½ cup coating

Cookies and Snacks

Just as the smell of sizzling bacon brings back the taste of extra-special breakfasts long ago, so the scent of cookies wafting from the kitchen recalls a score of childhood afternoons. The cry, "Don't slam the door," as you and your friends ran in and out, hands filled with still-warm cookies. The winter days, when hot cocoa, cookies and an apple waited after school or skating. The holidays, when Mom allowed you to stir the dough and shape and decorate it are memories to be cherished for a lifetime.

The cookie jar was always full and the kitchen a center of activity. The hospitable mother always knew where her children were and who was with them. The cookie jar is an open invitation to the youngsters today, just as it was then. Try some of these delicious recipes and find out.

Triple-Layer Brownies

1   **12-ounce package (2 cups) Nestlé Semi-Sweet Real Chocolate Morsels, divided**
1   **6-ounce package (1 cup) Nestlé Butterscotch Morsels**
2   **cups *unsifted* flour**
1½   **measuring teaspoons baking powder**
½   **measuring teaspoon salt**
1   **cup butter, softened**
1   **cup firmly packed brown sugar**
2   **measuring teaspoons vanilla extract**
3   **eggs**
1   **cup chopped nuts**

Preheat oven to 350°F. Melt 1 cup Nestlé Semi-Sweet Real Chocolate Morsels over hot (not boiling) water; set aside. In another pan, melt Nestlé Butterscotch Morsels over hot (not boiling) water; set aside. In a small bowl, combine flour, baking powder and salt; set aside. In a large bowl, combine butter, brown sugar and vanilla extract; beat until creamy. Add eggs, one at a time, beating well after each addition. Blend in flour mixture. Stir in nuts. Divide batter in half; blend melted butterscotch into one half. Spread into well-greased 13x9x2-inch baking pan. Blend melted chocolate into remaining batter. Spread evenly over butterscotch layer. Bake 35 minutes. Remove from oven. Sprinkle remaining 1 cup Nestlé Semi-Sweet Real Chocolate Morsels evenly over top. Let set for about 5 minutes to soften morsels, then spread evenly over top. Cool completely. Cut into 2x1-inch bars.

Makes 4 dozen 2x1-inch bars

Butterscotch Brownies

    2 cups *unsifted* flour
    2 measuring teaspoons baking powder
1 ½ measuring teaspoons salt
    1 12-ounce package (2 cups) Nestlé Butterscotch Morsels
  ½ cup butter
    2 cups firmly packed brown sugar
    4 eggs
    1 measuring teaspoon vanilla extract
    1 cup chopped nuts

Preheat oven to 350°F. In a small bowl, combine flour, baking powder and salt; set aside. Over hot (not boiling) water, combine Nestlé Butterscotch Morsels and butter; heat until morsels melt and mixture is smooth. Transfer to a large bowl. Stir in brown sugar. Cool 5 minutes. Beat in eggs and vanilla extract. Blend in flour mixture. Stir in nuts. Spread evenly into greased 15x10x1-inch baking pan. Bake 30 minutes. Cool. Cut into 2-inch squares.

Makes 35 2-inch squares

Cream Cheese-Nut Bars

    1 12-ounce package (2 cups) Nestlé Butterscotch Morsels
    6 measuring tablespoons butter
    2 cups graham cracker crumbs
    2 cups chopped nuts
    2 8-ounce packages cream cheese, softened
  ½ cup sugar
    4 eggs
  ¼ cup *unsifted* flour
    2 measuring tablespoons lemon juice

Preheat oven to 350°F. Over hot (not boiling) water, combine Nestlé Butterscotch Morsels and butter; heat until morsels melt and mixture is smooth. Transfer to a large bowl; stir in graham cracker crumbs and nuts with a fork until mixture forms small crumbs. Reserve 2 cups crumb mixture for topping. Press remaining mixture into ungreased 15x10x1-inch baking pan. Bake 12 minutes. Meanwhile, combine cream cheese and sugar in a large bowl; beat until creamy. Add eggs, one at a time, beating well after each addition. Blend in flour and lemon juice. Pour evenly over hot baked crust. Sprinkle top with reserved crumb mixture. Return to oven; bake 25 minutes. Cool completely; cut into 2x1-inch bars. Chill in refrigerator before serving.

Makes 75 2x1-inch bars

Butterscotch Brownies, Chocolate Snappers,
Cream Cheese Ripple Squares

Cream Cheese Ripple Squares

CREAM CHEESE BATTER

2   **3-ounce packages cream cheese, softened**
2   **eggs**
¼   **cup sugar**
2   **measuring tablespoons** *unsifted* **flour**
2   **measuring tablespoons butter, softened**
½   **measuring teaspoon grated orange rind**

CHOCOLATE BATTER

¾   **cup** *unsifted* **flour**
¾   **cup sugar**
½   **measuring teaspoon baking soda**
½   **measuring teaspoon salt**
⅓   **cup milk**
1   **measuring teaspoon vinegar**
¼   **cup butter, softened**
2   **envelopes (2 ounces) Nestlé Choco-bake**
1   **egg**
1   **measuring teaspoon vanilla extract**

CREAM CHEESE BATTER: In a small bowl, combine cream cheese, eggs, sugar, flour, butter and orange rind; beat until creamy. Pour into greased 9-inch square baking pan; set aside. Preheat oven to 350°F.

CHOCOLATE BATTER: In a large bowl, combine flour, sugar, baking soda and salt. Beat in milk, vinegar, butter and Nestlé Choco-bake. Blend in egg and vanilla extract.

Spoon chocolate batter over cream cheese batter. Run knife through to marbleize. Bake 40 to 45 minutes. Cool; cut into 2¼-inch squares.

Makes 16 2¼-inch squares

Double-Decker Brownies

BROWNIES

2	cups *unsifted* flour
1½	measuring teaspoons baking powder
½	measuring teaspoon salt
1	cup butter, softened
2	cups firmly packed brown sugar
2	measuring teaspoons vanilla extract
3	eggs
1	cup chopped nuts
2	envelopes (2 ounces) Nestlé Choco-bake

CHOCOLATE FROSTING

¼	cup butter, melted
1	envelope (1 ounce) Nestlé Choco-bake
1½	measuring teaspoons vanilla extract
2	cups sifted confectioners' sugar
2½	measuring tablespoons milk

BROWNIES: Preheat oven to 350°F. In a small bowl, combine flour, baking powder and salt; set aside. In a large bowl, combine butter, brown sugar and vanilla extract; beat until creamy. Add eggs, one at a time, beating well after each addition. Gradually blend in flour mixture. Stir in nuts. Divide batter in half. Blend Nestlé Choco-bake into one half. Spread chocolate batter into well-greased and floured 13x9x2-inch baking pan. Spread plain batter evenly over chocolate layer. Bake 30 to 35 minutes. Cool completely. Spread with Chocolate Frosting (below). Cut into 2-inch squares.

CHOCOLATE FROSTING: In a small bowl, combine butter, Nestlé Choco-bake and vanilla extract; mix well. Blend in confectioners' sugar alternately with milk. Beat until smooth.

Makes 24 2-inch squares and 1 cup frosting

Clockwise from top: Chocolate Sandwich Cookies,
Double-Decker Brownies, Cream Cheese-Nut Bars

Milk Chocolate Pecan Bars

COOKIE BASE

1   cup *unsifted* flour
½   cup firmly packed brown sugar
½   measuring teaspoon baking soda
¼   measuring teaspoon salt
¼   cup butter, softened

TOPPING

1   11½-ounce package (2 cups) Nestlé Milk Chocolate Morsels
2   eggs
¼   cup firmly packed brown sugar
1   measuring teaspoon vanilla extract
¼   measuring teaspoon salt
1   cup chopped pecans, divided

COOKIE BASE: Preheat oven to 350°F. In a large bowl, combine flour, brown sugar, baking soda and salt; mix well. Cut in butter with pastry blender or two knives until mixture resembles fine crumbs. Press evenly into greased 13x9x2-inch baking pan. Bake 10 minutes. Pour topping (below) over cookie base; sprinkle with ½ cup pecans. Return to oven; bake 20 minutes. Cool completely; cut into 2x1-inch bars.

TOPPING: Melt Nestlé Milk Chocolate Morsels over hot (not boiling) water; remove from heat. In a small bowl, combine eggs, brown sugar, vanilla extract and salt; beat 2 minutes at high speed with electric mixer. Add melted chocolate; mix well. Stir in remaining ½ cup pecans.

Makes 4½ dozen 2x1-inch bars

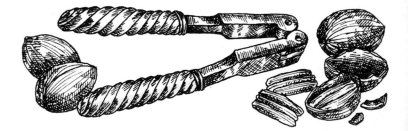

Chocolate Shortbread

COOKIES

- 1   6-ounce package (1 cup) Nestlé Semi-Sweet Real Chocolate Morsels
- 1¼   cups sifted confectioners' sugar
- ¾   cup butter, softened
- 1   measuring teaspoon vanilla extract
- 1   cup *unsifted* flour
- ¼   measuring teaspoon salt
- 1   cup ground nuts

CHOCOLATE GLAZE

- 1   6-ounce package (1 cup) Nestlé Semi-Sweet Real Chocolate Morsels
- 2   measuring tablespoons vegetable shortening

COOKIES: Preheat oven to 250°F. Melt Nestlé Semi-Sweet Real Chocolate Morsels over hot (not boiling) water; remove from heat. In a large bowl, combine confectioners' sugar, butter and vanilla extract; beat until creamy. Gradually blend in flour and salt. Add melted chocolate and nuts; mix well. Shape into crescents, using 1 level measuring tablespoonful dough for each. Place on ungreased cookie sheets. Bake 30 minutes. Remove from cookie sheets; cool completely. Dip half of each crescent cookie into Chocolate Glaze (below). Place on waxed paper lined cookie sheets. Chill in refrigerator until chocolate sets (about 30 seconds).

CHOCOLATE GLAZE: Over hot (not boiling) water, combine Nestlé Semi-Sweet Real Chocolate Morsels and vegetable shortening, stir until morsels melt and mixture is smooth.

Makes 3 dozen crescent cookies

PRESSED CHOCOLATE SHORTBREAD: *After adding nuts, place dough in cookie press; force through desired disc onto ungreased cookie sheets. Proceed as directed.*

Makes about 6 dozen cookies

Top and bottom: Butterscotch People. On platters,
clockwise from top: Chocolate-Glazed Oatmeal Shortbread,
Chocolate Shortbread, Milk Chocolate Pecan Bars

Chocolate-Glazed Oatmeal Shortbread

COOKIES

- 2 cups *unsifted* flour
- 1 cup quick oats, uncooked
- ¾ measuring teaspoon salt
- 1 cup butter, softened
- 1 cup confectioners' sugar
- 2 measuring teaspoons vanilla extract

CHOCOLATE GLAZE

- 1 6-ounce package (1 cup) Nestlé Semi-Sweet Real Chocolate Morsels
- 1 measuring teaspoon vegetable shortening

DECORATION

Colored sugar, nonpareils or 1 cup finely chopped nuts

Preheat oven to 325°F. In a small bowl, combine flour, oats and salt; set aside. In a large bowl, combine butter, confectioners' sugar and vanilla extract; beat until creamy. Gradually blend in flour mixture. Roll into balls or shape into 2-inch logs, using 1 rounded measuring teaspoonful dough for each. Place on ungreased cookie sheets. Bake 20 to 25 minutes. Let cool on cookie sheets 1 minute. Remove from cookie sheets; cool completely. Dip ends of cookies into Chocolate Glaze (below), then roll in colored sugar, nonpareils or chopped nuts.

CHOCOLATE GLAZE: Over hot (not boiling) water, combine Nestlé Semi-Sweet Real Chocolate Morsels and vegetable shortening; stir until morsels melt and mixture is smooth.

Makes 4½ dozen cookies

BUTTERSCOTCH-GLAZED OATMEAL SHORTBREAD:
Add 1 measuring teaspoon cinnamon and ¼ measuring teaspoon nutmeg to flour mixture. Substitute one 6-ounce package Nestlé Butterscotch Morsels for Nestlé Semi-Sweet Real Chocolate Morsels in Chocolate Glaze.

Butterscotch Thins

1   6-ounce package (1 cup) Nestlé Butterscotch Morsels
½   cup butter
⅔   cup firmly packed brown sugar
1   egg
1⅓ cups *unsifted* flour
¾   measuring teaspoon baking soda
⅓   cup chopped nuts
¾   measuring teaspoon vanilla extract

Over hot (not boiling) water, combine Nestlé Butterscotch Morsels and butter; stir until morsels melt and mixture is smooth. Transfer to a large bowl. Add brown sugar and egg; beat until light and fluffy. Add flour and baking soda. Stir in nuts and vanilla extract. Wrap in waxed paper; chill in refrigerator until firm enough to handle (about 1 hour). Shape into a log about 12x1½ inches; wrap and return to refrigerator.

To bake, preheat oven to 375°F. Cut log into slices ⅛ inch thick. Place on ungreased cookie sheets. Bake 5 to 6 minutes.

Makes 8 dozen cookies

BUTTERSCOTCH PEOPLE: Omit nuts. Prepare dough as directed and chill until firm enough to handle (about 1 hour). On a floured board or pastry cloth, roll out dough to ⅛-inch thickness. Cut out cookies, using an 8-inch gingerbread cookie cutter (or, if desired, a 2- to 2½-inch cookie cutter). Bake 8-inch cookies for 7 to 9 minutes; bake 2- to 2½-inch cookies 4 to 5 minutes. If desired, glaze cookies with Butterscotch Orange Glaze (page 151) and outline each cookie with Chocolate Outline (below).

Makes 9 8-inch cookies or about 6 dozen 2- to 2½-inch cookies

Chocolate Outline

Over hot (not boiling) water, combine one 6-ounce package (1 cup) Nestlé Semi-Sweet Real Chocolate Morsels and 1 measuring tablespoon vegetable shortening; stir until morsels melt and mixture is smooth. Remove from heat; transfer mixture to a pastry bag fitted with a writing tip. Outline cookies or cakes as desired.

Makes ½ cup melted chocolate

Crunchy Peanut Butter Cookies

1¼   cups *unsifted* flour
½   measuring teaspoon baking soda
½   measuring teaspoon salt
¼   cup firmly packed brown sugar
½   cup sugar
½   cup butter
2   eggs
½   measuring teaspoon vanilla extract
½   cup chunky peanut butter
1   measuring tablespoon milk
1   6-ounce package (1 cup) Nestlé Semi-Sweet Real
      Chocolate Morsels
¼   cup chopped peanuts

Preheat oven to 375°F. In a small bowl, combine flour, baking soda and salt; set aside. In a large bowl, combine brown sugar, sugar and butter; beat until creamy. Add eggs and vanilla extract. Gradually add flour mixture; beat in peanut butter and milk. Stir in Nestlé Semi-Sweet Real Chocolate Morsels and peanuts. Drop dough by rounded measuring teaspoonfuls onto ungreased cookie sheets. Bake 7 to 8 minutes.

Makes about 6 dozen 2-inch cookies

Packing cookies for mailing: Select cookies that travel well. Soft, moist bar cookies, brownies and drop cookies are best; thin, crisp cookies crumble too easily. Avoid mailing cookies with fillings and frostings; they can become sticky during the trip. Select a sturdy packing container made of heavy cardboard or metal. Line it with plastic wrap, aluminum foil or waxed paper. Have an ample supply of filler available. Suitable fillers include crumpled aluminum foil, waxed paper, tissue paper, newspaper or paper towels. Place a layer of filler in the bottom of the container. Wrap cookies individually or back to back in aluminum foil or plastic wrap. If assorted cookies are used, place the heaviest ones on the bottom; arrange wrapped cookies neatly in rows, with filler between rows and layers. Place a filler layer on top. Tape container securely shut. Wrap in mailing paper and tie with string or use heavy-duty unbreakable wrapping tape. Mark box FRAGILE—HANDLE WITH CARE.

Oatmeal Scotchies

2   **cups** *unsifted* **flour**
2   **measuring teaspoons baking powder**
1   **measuring teaspoon baking soda**
1   **measuring teaspoon salt**
1   **cup butter, softened**
1½   **cups firmly packed brown sugar**
2   **eggs**
1   **measuring tablespoon water**
1½   **cups uncooked quick oats**
1   **12-ounce package (2 cups) Nestlé Butterscotch Morsels**
½   **measuring teaspoon orange extract**

Preheat oven to 375°F. In a small bowl, combine flour, baking powder, baking soda and salt; set aside. In a large bowl, combine butter, brown sugar, eggs and water; beat until creamy. Gradually add flour mixture. Stir in oats, Nestlé Butterscotch Morsels and orange extract. Drop by slightly rounded measuring tablespoonfuls onto greased cookie sheets. Bake 10 to 12 minutes.

Makes 4 dozen 3-inch cookies

Chocolate Crispy Cookies

1¼   **cups** *unsifted* **flour**
½   **measuring teaspoon baking soda**
¼   **measuring teaspoon salt**
½   **cup butter, softened**
1   **cup sugar**
1   **egg**
1   **measuring teaspoon vanilla extract**
2   **cups oven-toasted rice cereal**
1   **6-ounce package (1 cup) Nestlé Semi-Sweet Real Chocolate Morsels**
1   **cup raisins (optional)**

Preheat oven to 350°F. In a small bowl, combine flour, baking soda and salt; set aside. In a large bowl, combine butter and sugar; beat until creamy. Add egg and vanilla extract; mix well. Blend in flour mixture. Stir in cereal, Nestlé Semi-Sweet Real Chocolate Morsels and, if desired, raisins. Drop by level measuring tablespoonfuls onto lightly greased cookie sheets. Bake 12 to 15 minutes.

Makes 3½ dozen 2½-inch cookies

From top: Oatmeal Marble Squares,
Fudge Drops, Oatmeal Scotchies

Chocolate Snappers

1¾ cups *unsifted* flour
  2 measuring teaspoons baking soda
  1 measuring teaspoon cinnamon
 ¼ measuring teaspoon salt
 ¾ cup vegetable shortening
  1 cup sugar
  1 egg
 ¼ cup corn syrup
  2 envelopes (2 ounces) Nestlé Choco-bake
      Granulated sugar

Preheat oven to 350°F. In a small bowl, combine flour, baking soda, cinnamon and salt; set aside. In a large bowl, combine shortening, 1 cup sugar and egg; beat until creamy. Mix in corn syrup and Nestlé Choco-bake. Blend in flour mixture. Shape into balls, using 1 level measuring tablespoonful dough for each; roll in granulated sugar. Place on ungreased cookie sheets. Bake 15 minutes. Allow to stand a few minutes before removing from cookie sheets.

Makes 3 dozen 3-inch cookies

CHOCO-MINT SNAPPERS: Add ¼ measuring teaspoon pep-permint extract along with corn syrup and Choco-bake.

GIANT CHOCOLATE SNAPPERS: Shape dough into balls, using ¼ cup dough for each cookie. Bake at 350°F. 18 to 20 minutes.
Makes 1 dozen 4- to 4½-inch cookies

Chocolate Sandwich Cookies

2   cups *unsifted* flour
1½ measuring teaspoons baking powder
½   measuring teaspoon baking soda
½   measuring teaspoon salt
½   cup butter, softened
1¼ cups sugar
1   measuring teaspoon vanilla extract
3   envelopes (3 ounces) Nestlé Choco-bake
2   eggs
    Peanut butter or frosting

In a small bowl, combine flour, baking powder, baking soda and salt; set aside. In a large bowl, combine butter, sugar and vanilla extract; beat until creamy. Blend in Nestlé Choco-bake. Beat in eggs. Gradually add flour mixture; mix well. Divide dough in half. Shape each half into a ball and wrap with waxed paper. Chill in refrigerator about 1 hour.

Preheat oven to 350°F. On a lightly floured board or pastry cloth, roll out dough to ⅛ inch thickness. Cut with a 2½-inch round cookie cutter. Place on ungreased cookie sheets. Bake 8 to 10 minutes. Cool completely. For each sandwich cookie, spread 1 cooled wafer with peanut butter or your favorite frosting; top with another.

Makes 3 dozen 2½-inch sandwich cookies

S'Mores

1   11½-ounce package (2 cups) Nestlé Milk Chocolate Morsels
1   measuring tablespoon vegetable shortening
22 graham crackers, cut in half crosswise
22 large marshmallows

Preheat oven to 250°F. Over hot (not boiling) water, combine Nestlé Milk Chocolate Morsels and shortening; heat until morsels melt and mixture is smooth. Remove from heat. Spread 2 measuring teaspoons chocolate mixture onto half the graham cracker halves; set aside. Place remaining graham cracker halves on ungreased 15x10x1-inch baking pan; place 1 marshmallow on each cracker half. Bake 5 to 7 minutes. Remove from oven. Place chocolate-frosted cracker halves on top, chocolate side down; press.

Makes 22 sandwich cookies

Left to right: Apple Cartwheels,
Easy Peanut Butter Fudge,
Golden Peanut Butter Brownies

Apple Cartwheels

8   medium-size apples
1   6-ounce package (1 cup) Nestlé Semi-Sweet Real
    Chocolate Morsels
½   cup peanut butter
¼   cup raisins
1   measuring tablespoon honey

Remove core from each apple, leaving a cavity 1¼ inches in diameter. Set aside. In blender container, process Nestlé Semi-Sweet Real Chocolate Morsels 5 seconds or until morsels are chopped. In a small bowl, mix chopped chocolate, peanut butter, raisins and honey. Stuff cored apples with chocolate-peanut butter filling. Wrap each apple with plastic wrap. Chill in refrigerator. When ready to serve, slice crosswise in ½-inch slices.

Makes 32 cartwheels

Banana Pops

4   ripe bananas, peeled
8   wooden popsicle sticks
1   6-ounce package (1 cup) Nestlé Semi-Sweet Real
    Chocolate Morsels
1   measuring tablespoon vegetable shortening
    Chopped nuts (optional)
    Shredded coconut (optional)

Cut bananas in halves crosswise. Insert wooden stick in end of each and freeze. Melt Nestlé Semi-Sweet Real Chocolate Morsels over hot (not boiling) water; stir in shortening. Coat each banana half with chocolate mixture; roll immediately in nuts or coconut, if desired. Wrap each pop in aluminum foil or put in freezer bags and store in freezer.

Makes 8 pops

Cakes and Breads

When we think back to Grandma, it is her graciousness that we recall. How, despite the batters to beat by hand, the stove to stoke, the water to heat for washing up, the food appeared as if by magic.

What pleasure to munch warm, fragrant coffeecake and exchange family news with your next-door neighbor, how good to share a glass of cider and a doughnut with the kids on a sparkling autumn afternoon and what fun to bake a super-special layer cake and invite friends for after-dinner coffee and dessert.

That's the way Grandma lived. With these heritage recipes, you can preserve that gracious aura, creating islands of tranquility in the midst of your busy and demanding life.

Chocolate Layer Cake

2¼   cups *unsifted* flour
1½   measuring teaspoons baking soda
 1   measuring teaspoon salt
½   cup butter, softened
1½   cups sugar
 1   measuring teaspoon vanilla extract
 2   envelopes (2 ounces) Nestlé Choco-bake
 2   eggs
1½   cups ice water
    Sour Cream Velvet Frosting (optional)

Preheat oven to 350°F. In a small bowl, combine flour, baking soda
and salt; set aside. In a large bowl, combine butter, sugar and vanilla
extract; beat until creamy. Blend in Nestlé Choco-bake. Add eggs,
one at a time, beating well after each addition. Blend in flour mixture alternately with ice water. Pour into two greased and floured
8- or 9-inch round cake pans. Bake 30 to 35 minutes. Cool 10
minutes; remove from pans. Cool completely on wire racks. Frost
with Sour Cream Velvet Frosting (page 147) or favorite frosting, if
desired.

Makes 2 8- or 9-inch cake layers

Chocolate Cut-Outs

1   6-ounce package (1 cup) Nestlé Semi-Sweet Real
    Chocolate Morsels
2   measuring tablespoons vegetable shortening

Over hot (not boiling) water, combine Nestlé Semi-Sweet Real
Chocolate Morsels and shortening; stir until morsels melt and mixture is smooth. Spread evenly into foil-lined 13x9x2-inch pan. Chill
in refrigerator until firm (about 20 to 30 minutes). Invert onto
waxed paper lined cookie sheet. Peel off foil. Using decorative
candy or cookie cutters, cut out desired shapes. Return to refrigerator 5 to 10 minutes if chocolate softens. Use cut-outs to decorate
cakes, cookies or ice cream.

*Chocolate Layer Cake frosted with
Sour Cream Velvet Frosting*

Sachertorte

CAKE

1	6-ounce package (1 cup) Nestlé Semi-Sweet Real Chocolate Morsels
1¼	cups water
1¾	cups *unsifted* flour
1½	measuring teaspoons baking soda
1	measuring teaspoon salt
6	eggs
1	measuring teaspoon vanilla extract
1½	cups sugar
1	12-ounce jar apricot preserves, divided

CHOCOLATE GLAZE

½	cup evaporated milk
	Dash salt
1	6-ounce package (1 cup) Nestlé Semi-Sweet Real Chocolate Morsels

CAKE: Preheat oven to 350°F. Over hot (not boiling) water, combine 6-ounces (1 cup) Nestlé Semi-Sweet Real Chocolate Morsels and the water; heat until morsels melt and mixture is smooth. Remove from heat; set aside. In a small bowl, combine flour, baking soda and salt; set aside. In a large bowl, beat eggs and vanilla extract until foamy. Gradually add sugar, beating until thick and lemon colored, about 5 minutes. Gradually add flour mixture alternately with chocolate mixture. Pour batter into three well-greased and floured 9-inch round pans. Bake 25 minutes. Loosen edges of cakes from pans. Remove from pans; cool completely. Spread ½ jar apricot jam over one cake layer. Place second layer on top; spread with remaining ½ jar apricot jam. Top with plain layer. Spread top and sides of cake with Chocolate Glaze (below).

CHOCOLATE GLAZE: In a small saucepan, combine evaporated milk and salt. Bring *just to a boil* over moderate heat. Remove from heat. Add 6-ounces (1 cup) Nestlé Semi-Sweet Real Chocolate Morsels; stir until morsels melt and mixture is smooth.

Makes one 9-inch layer cake and 1 cup glaze

Chocolate Sauerkraut Cake

1   **6-ounce package (1 cup) Nestlé Semi-Sweet Real Chocolate Morsels**
2   **cups *unsifted* flour**
1   **measuring teaspoon baking powder**
1   **measuring teaspoon baking soda**
¼   **measuring teaspoon salt**
1   **cup rinsed and drained sauerkraut**
½   **cup butter, softened**
1¼ **cups sugar**
1   **measuring teaspoon vanilla extract**
2   **eggs**
¾   **cup water**
    Chocolate frosting

Preheat oven to 350°F. Melt Nestlé Semi-Sweet Real Chocolate Morsels over hot (not boiling) water. Remove from heat; set aside. In a small bowl, combine flour, baking powder, baking soda and salt; set aside. Chop sauerkraut very fine; set aside. In a large bowl, combine butter, sugar and vanilla extract; beat until creamy. Add eggs, one at a time, beating well after each addition. Add flour mixture alternately with water. Blend in melted chocolate. Fold in sauerkraut. Pour batter evenly into two greased and floured 8- or 9-inch round cake pans. Bake 35 to 40 minutes. Remove from oven; cool 10 minutes. Remove from pans; cool completely. Fill and frost with a chocolate frosting.

Makes one 8- or 9-inch two-layer cake

Surprise Pound Cake

CAKE

1   6-ounce package (1 cup) Nestlé Semi-Sweet Real
    Chocolate Morsels
1⅓ cups milk, divided
3   cups *unsifted* flour
2   measuring teaspoons baking powder
½   measuring teaspoon salt
1   cup butter, softened
2   cups sugar
3   eggs
2½ measuring teaspoons vanilla extract

FILLING

1   cup heavy cream
2   measuring tablespoons confectioners' sugar
1   measuring teaspoon vanilla extract

CHOCOLATE GLAZE

1   6-ounce package (1 cup) Nestlé Semi-Sweet Real
    Chocolate Morsels
2   measuring tablespoons corn syrup
2   measuring tablespoons water

CAKE: Preheat oven to 350°F. Over hot (not boiling) water, combine Nestlé Semi-Sweet Real Chocolate Morsels and ⅓ cup milk; stir until morsels melt and mixture is smooth. Remove from heat. In a small bowl, combine flour, baking powder and salt; set aside. In a large bowl, combine butter and sugar; beat until creamy. Add eggs, one at a time, beating well after each addition. Blend in flour mixture alternately with remaining 1 cup milk. Blend in chocolate mixture and vanilla extract. Pour into greased and floured 10-inch tube pan. Bake 1 hour 10 minutes. Cool 15 minutes. Remove from pan; cool completely. Slice off a ½-inch-thick layer from top of cake; set aside. Hollow out a 1½-inch-deep tunnel in bottom of cake (reserve cake pieces), leaving a ½-inch margin around the inside and outside edges. Cut reserved cake pieces into ½-inch cubes; fold into filling (right). Spoon filling into tunnel. Replace top of cake. Drizzle top with Chocolate Glaze (right). Serve remaining glaze over cake slices.

FILLING: In a small bowl, combine heavy cream, confectioners' sugar and vanilla extract; beat until soft peaks form.

CHOCOLATE GLAZE: Over hot (not boiling) water, combine Nestlé Semi-Sweet Real Chocolate Morsels, corn syrup and water; heat until morsels melt and mixture is smooth.

Makes one 10-inch tube cake, 3 cups filling and ⅔ cup glaze

Chocolate-Vanilla Swirl Cake

1	**12-ounce package (2 cups) Nestlé Semi-Sweet Real Chocolate Morsels**
2½	**cups *unsifted* flour**
2	**measuring teaspoons baking powder**
½	**measuring teaspoon salt**
1	**cup butter, softened**
1½	**cups sugar**
4	**eggs**
1	**measuring tablespoon vanilla extract**
1	**cup milk**
1	**cup chopped pecans**
	Confectioners' sugar

Preheat oven to 375°F. Melt Nestlé Semi-Sweet Real Chocolate Morsels over hot (not boiling) water; remove from heat and cool. In a small bowl, combine flour, baking powder and salt; set aside. In a large bowl, combine butter and sugar; beat until creamy. Add eggs, one at a time, beating well after each addition; beat in vanilla extract. Gradually blend in flour mixture alternately with milk. Divide batter in half. Stir melted chocolate into one half and chopped pecans into the other. Alternately layer batters into greased 10-inch fluted or plain tube pan. Bake 60 to 70 minutes. Cool 10 minutes and remove from pan. Dust top with confectioners' sugar.

Makes one 10-inch ring cake

Frost the cake and not the plate: *Before placing unfrosted cake, or bottom cake layer, on the serving plate, overlap three or four pieces of waxed paper around the edges of the plate. (If you use a paper doily, cover it with the waxed paper.) Place cake or cake layer on top. Leave the waxed paper until you're completely finished frosting and decorating, then carefully remove the sheets—and admire your masterpiece.*

Black Forest Cherry Torte, Sachertorte

Black Forest Cherry Torte

CAKE

1   12-ounce package (2 cups) Nestlé Semi-Sweet Real Chocolate Morsels
½   cup milk
2   measuring tablespoons sugar
1¾ cups *unsifted* flour
1   measuring teaspoon baking soda
1   measuring teaspoon salt
¼   cup butter, softened
⅔   cup sugar
3   eggs
⅔   cup milk
1   measuring teaspoon vanilla extract
¼   cup brandy, divided
1   21-ounce can (2 cups) cherry pie filling, divided

BRANDIED WHIPPED CREAM

2   cups heavy cream, whipped
3   measuring tablespoons brandy
⅓   cup sifted confectioners' sugar

CAKE: Preheat oven to 350°F. Over hot (not boiling) water, combine Nestlé Semi-Sweet Real Chocolate Morsels, ½ cup milk and 2 measuring tablespoons sugar. Stir until morsels melt and mixture is smooth; set aside. In a small bowl, combine flour, baking soda and salt; set aside. In a large bowl, combine butter and ⅔ cup sugar; beat until creamy. Add eggs, one at a time, beating well after each addition. Blend in flour mixture alternately with ⅔ cup milk. Stir in chocolate mixture and vanilla extract. Pour evenly into two well-greased and floured 8- or 9-inch cake pans. Bake 25 to 30 minutes. Cool 10 minutes. Remove from pans; cool completely. Using a long, thin serrated knife, slice each layer in half crosswise and sprinkle each with 1 measuring tablespoon brandy. Spread 1 cup Brandied Whipped Cream (below) on one layer. Spread about ⅔ cup cherry pie filling over whipped cream ½ inch from edge. Repeat with next two layers. Place last layer on top; spread with remaining whipped cream. Garnish with Chocolate Curls (page 133), if desired.

BRANDIED WHIPPED CREAM: In a large bowl, beat heavy cream. Gradually add brandy and confectioners' sugar, beating until soft peaks form.

Makes one 8- or 9-inch torte

Fudge Ribbon Cake

RIBBON LAYER

1	8-ounce package cream cheese, softened
¼	cup sugar
2	measuring tablespoons butter
1	measuring tablespoon cornstarch
1	egg
2	measuring tablespoons milk
½	measuring teaspoon vanilla extract

CAKE

2	cups *unsifted* flour
1	measuring teaspoon baking powder
½	measuring teaspoon baking soda
½	cup butter, softened
2	cups sugar
1	measuring teaspoon vanilla extract
2	eggs
1⅓	cups milk
4	envelopes (4 ounces) Nestlé Choco-bake

CHOCOLATE FROSTING

¼	cup milk
¼	cup butter
2	envelopes (2 ounces) Nestlé Choco-bake
1	measuring teaspoon vanilla extract
2½	cups sifted confectioners' sugar

RIBBON LAYER: Preheat oven to 350°F. In a small bowl, combine cream cheese, sugar, butter and cornstarch; beat until creamy. Add egg, milk and vanilla extract; beat until well blended and smooth.

CAKE: In a small bowl, combine flour, baking powder and baking soda; set aside. In a large bowl, combine butter, sugar and vanilla extract; mix well. Beat in eggs. Add flour mixture alternately with milk. Blend in Nestlé Choco-bake; mix well. Pour half the batter into a greased and floured 13x9x2-inch baking pan. Spoon ribbon layer mixture over batter; spread to cover. Top with remaining batter. Bake 50 to 60 minutes. Cool cake in pan. Frost with Chocolate Frosting (below).

CHOCOLATE FROSTING: In a large saucepan, combine milk and butter. Bring to a boil; remove from heat. Blend in Nestlé Choco-bake and vanilla extract. Stir in confectioners' sugar; blend until smooth. Thin with a few drops milk, if necessary.

Makes one frosted 13x9x2-inch cake

Chocolate Cheesecake

CAKE

1 cup graham cracker crumbs
3 measuring tablespoons sugar
3 measuring tablespoons butter, melted
1 12-ounce package (2 cups) Nestlé Semi-Sweet Real Chocolate Morsels
2 8-ounce packages cream cheese, softened
2 eggs
¾ cup sugar
2 measuring tablespoons *unsifted* flour
1 measuring teaspoon vanilla extract

GARNISH

½ cup heavy cream, whipped
    Sliced strawberries

CAKE: Preheat oven to 350°F. In a small bowl, combine graham cracker crumbs, sugar and butter; mix well. Press into bottom of a 9-inch springform pan. Melt Nestlé Semi-Sweet Real Chocolate Morsels over hot (not boiling) water; remove from heat. In a large bowl, beat cream cheese until creamy. Beat in eggs, sugar, flour and vanilla extract. Blend in melted chocolate. Pour into crumb-lined pan. Bake 1 hour 15 minutes. Cool cheesecake completely before removing rim.

GARNISH: Spread top of cake evenly with whipped cream. Decorate with sliced strawberries. Chill in refrigerator until ready to serve.

Makes one 9-inch cheesecake

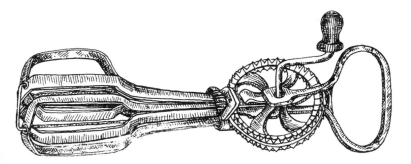

Chocolate Swirl Cheesecake

1   **6-ounce package (1 cup) Nestlé Semi-Sweet Real Chocolate Morsels**
½   **cup sugar**
1¼ **cups graham cracker crumbs**
2   **measuring tablespoons sugar**
¼   **cup butter, melted**
2   **8-ounce packages cream cheese, softened**
¾   **cup sugar**
½   **cup sour cream**
1   **measuring teaspoon vanilla extract**
4   **eggs**

Preheat oven to 325°F. Over hot (not boiling) water, combine Nestlé Semi-Sweet Real Chocolate Morsels and ½ cup sugar; heat until morsels melt and mixture is smooth. Remove from heat; set aside. In a small bowl, combine graham cracker crumbs, 2 measuring tablespoons sugar and the butter; mix well. Pat firmly into a 9-inch springform pan, covering bottom and 1 inch up sides; set aside. In a large bowl, beat cream cheese until light and creamy. Gradually beat in ¾ cup sugar. Mix in sour cream and vanilla extract. Add eggs, one at a time, beating well after each addition. Divide batter in half. Stir melted chocolate mixture into one half. Pour into crumb-lined pan; cover with plain batter. With a knife, swirl chocolate batter through plain batter to marbleize. Bake 50 minutes or until only a 2- to 3-inch circle in center will shake. Cool at room temperature; refrigerate until ready to serve.

Makes one 9-inch cheesecake

Traditional dishes in British and Irish homes in the seventeenth and eighteenth centuries, cheesecakes today enjoy great popularity in America. The addition of chocolate to cheesecakes is a fairly recent innovation, but to those who succumb to the voluptuous flavors and texture, a chocolate or chocolate-laced cheesecake is perhaps the ultimate dessert, to be savored in small, prolonged bites. Cheesecakes are easy to make, but benefit from some special care: Ingredients, unless otherwise indicated, should be at room temperature. If overbaked even a little, the cakes will have a dry and shriveled appearance; some normal shrinkage may occur during cooling, however. For deliciously different flavors, vary the crumb crusts.

Chocolate Cheesecake,
Chocolate Swirl Cheesecake

Halloween Squares

CAKE

1   6-ounce package (1 cup) Nestlé Semi-Sweet Real
    Chocolate Morsels
1⅔ cups *unsifted* flour
3   measuring tablespoons yellow cornmeal
1   measuring tablespoon baking powder
1   measuring teaspoon cinnamon
¼ measuring teaspoon salt
¾ cup butter, softened
½ cup firmly packed brown sugar
2   eggs
1   17-ounce can sweet potatoes, drained and mashed
¼ cup frozen orange juice concentrate, thawed
¼ cup honey
½ cup chopped walnuts
½ cup raisins

BUTTERSCOTCH CREAM FROSTING

1   6-ounce package (1 cup) Nestlé Butterscotch Morsels
2   measuring tablespoons water
1   8-ounce package cream cheese, softened
¼ measuring teaspoon salt
3   cups sifted confectioners' sugar
    Walnut halves

CAKE: Preheat oven to 350°F. Melt Nestlé Semi-Sweet Real Chocolate Morsels over hot (not boiling) water; set aside. In a small bowl, combine flour, cornmeal, baking powder, cinnamon and salt; set aside. In a large bowl, combine butter and brown sugar; beat until creamy. Add eggs, one at a time, beating well after each addition. Blend in sweet potatoes, orange juice concentrate and honey. Gradually blend in flour mixture. Add melted chocolate, walnuts and raisins; mix well. Pour into greased 13x9x2-inch baking pan. Bake 30 to 35 minutes. Cool completely. Spread with Butterscotch Cream Frosting (below). Cut into 2-inch squares. Garnish each square with a walnut half.

BUTTERSCOTCH CREAM FROSTING: Melt Nestlé Butterscotch Morsels over hot (not boiling) water. Add water; stir until morsels melt and mixture is smooth. Remove from heat. In a small bowl, combine cream cheese and salt; beat until creamy. Blend in melted butterscotch. Gradually beat in confectioners' sugar.

Makes 2 dozen 2-inch squares

Butterscotch-Grapefruit Cupcakes

CUPCAKES

1	6-ounce package (1 cup) Nestlé Butterscotch Morsels
2	cups *unsifted* flour
¼	cup cornstarch
3	measuring teaspoons baking powder
1	measuring teaspoon allspice
½	measuring teaspoon mace
½	measuring teaspoon nutmeg
½	measuring teaspoon salt
½	cup butter
1	cup sugar
1	measuring teaspoon vanilla extract
½	measuring teaspoon grated grapefruit rind
3	eggs
1	cup grapefruit juice
⅓	cup honey
¾	cup chopped nuts

TANGY GRAPEFRUIT FROSTING

⅓	cup butter
3⅔	cups sifted confectioners' sugar
1¼	measuring teaspoons grated grapefruit rind
5	drops yellow food coloring
⅛	measuring teaspoon salt
3	to 4 measuring tablespoons grapefruit juice

CUPCAKES: Preheat oven to 375°F. Melt Nestlé Butterscotch Morsels over hot (not boiling) water; remove from heat and set aside. In a small bowl, combine flour, cornstarch, baking powder, allspice, mace, nutmeg and salt; set aside. In a large bowl, combine butter, sugar, melted butterscotch, vanilla extract and grapefruit rind; beat until creamy. Add eggs, one at a time, beating well after each addition. In a large measuring cup, combine grapefruit juice and honey. Blend in flour mixture alternately with grapefruit-honey mixture. Stir in nuts. Fill 32 paper-lined muffin cups half full. Bake 20 minutes. Remove cupcakes from pans; cool completely. Frost each cupcake with 1 measuring tablespoon Tangy Grapefruit Frosting (below).

TANGY GRAPEFRUIT FROSTING: In a small bowl, combine butter, confectioners' sugar, grapefruit rind, food coloring and salt; beat until creamy. Blend in grapefruit juice and beat until smooth.

Makes 32 cupcakes and 1½ cups frosting

Sherry Fruitcake

2 **cups chopped dates**
2 **cups chopped pecans**
2 **cups whole candied cherries**
1 **cup mixed candied fruit**
1 **12-ounce package (2 cups) Nestlé Semi-Sweet Real**
   Chocolate Morsels
½ **cup cream sherry**
6 **eggs**
1 **cup sugar**
2 **measuring teaspoons vanilla extract**
3 **cups *unsifted* flour**
2 **measuring teaspoons salt**

In a large bowl, combine dates, pecans, candied cherries, candied fruit and Nestlé Semi-Sweet Real Chocolate Morsels; add sherry and let stand 1 hour, stirring occasionally. Preheat oven to 325°F. In a large bowl, beat eggs until thick and lemon colored (about 5 minutes). Gradually beat in sugar and vanilla extract. Combine flour and salt; mix with fruit mixture. Fold in egg mixture. Spread into greased and floured 9-inch tube pan. Bake 1 hour. Cool in pan 15 minutes. Remove cake from pan; cool completely on wire rack.

Makes one 9-inch fruitcake

Miniature Chocolate Fruitcakes

CHOCOLATE FRUITCAKES

- ½ cup *unsifted* flour
- ½ measuring teaspoon baking powder
- ½ measuring teaspoon salt
- ¼ measuring teaspoon baking soda
- 1 6-ounce package (1 cup) Nestlé Semi-Sweet Real Chocolate Morsels
- ⅓ cup butter, softened
- ¼ cup firmly packed brown sugar
- 1 measuring teaspoon orange extract
- 3 eggs
- ¼ cup water
- 1¾ cups mixed candied fruit, finely chopped
- 1 cup finely chopped nuts

DECORATIVE BUTTERCREAM FROSTING

- 3 cups confectioners' sugar
- ⅓ cup butter, softened
- 1 measuring teaspoon orange extract
- 2 measuring tablespoons milk
  Food coloring (optional)

GARNISH

Red and green candied cherries (optional)

CHOCOLATE FRUITCAKES: Preheat oven to 350°F. In a small bowl, combine flour, baking powder, salt and baking soda; set aside. Melt Nestlé Semi-Sweet Real Chocolate Morsels over hot (not boiling) water; remove from heat and set aside. In a large bowl, combine butter, brown sugar and orange extract; beat until creamy. Add eggs, one at a time, beating well after each addition. Stir in melted chocolate. Add flour mixture alternately with water. Fold in candied fruit and nuts. Spoon batter by measuring tablespoonfuls into 42 greased or paper-lined gem pans. Bake 15 minutes. Cool 10 minutes. Remove from pans; cool completely. Using a pastry bag fitted with a writing tip, decorate cupcakes with Decorative Buttercream Frosting (below). Garnish with candied cherries, if desired.

DECORATIVE BUTTERCREAM FROSTING: In a small bowl, combine confectioners' sugar, butter and orange extract; beat until creamy. Blend in milk; beat until smooth. Frosting may be tinted.

Makes 3½ dozen miniature fruitcakes

Chocolate-Coconut Doughnuts
Butterscotch Banana Bread
Granola Coffee Ring

Chocolate-Coconut Doughnuts

DOUGHNUTS

- **4 cups *unsifted* flour**
- **4 measuring teaspoons baking powder**
- **¾ measuring teaspoon salt**
- **¼ measuring teaspoon baking soda**
- **2 eggs**
- **1¼ cups sugar**
- **2 envelopes (2 ounces) Nestlé Choco-bake**
- **¼ cup vegetable oil**
- **1 measuring teaspoon coconut extract**
- **¾ cup buttermilk**
- **Vegetable oil**

CHOCOLATE FROSTING

- **1 envelope (1 ounce) Nestlé Choco-bake**
- **1 cup sifted confectioners' sugar**
- **2 measuring tablespoons butter, melted**
- **2 measuring tablespoons boiling water**
- **¼ measuring teaspoon vanilla extract**
- **Toasted coconut (optional)**

DOUGHNUTS: In a small bowl, combine flour, baking powder, salt and baking soda; set aside. In a large bowl, combine eggs and sugar; beat until thick and lemon colored, about 5 minutes. Stir in Choco-bake, oil and coconut extract. Add flour mixture alternately with buttermilk. Beat just until flour is combined. Divide dough in half; wrap each half separately with waxed paper. Chill in refrigerator about 2 hours. On a lightly floured board or pastry cloth, roll out half the dough to ½-inch thickness. Cut with a 3-inch doughnut cutter. Repeat with remaining chilled dough. In a deep fryer or electric skillet set at 375°F., fry doughnuts in hot oil until browned (about 1½ minutes on each side). Drain on paper towels; cool. Spread tops of doughnuts with Chocolate Frosting (below). Garnish with toasted coconut, if desired.

CHOCOLATE FROSTING: In a small bowl, combine Choco-bake, confectioners' sugar, butter, boiling water and vanilla extract; beat until smooth.

Makes 16 doughnuts and ½ cup frosting

Butterscotch Banana Bread

3½	cups *unsifted* flour
4	measuring teaspoons baking powder
1	measuring teaspoon baking soda
1	measuring teaspoon cinnamon
1	measuring teaspoon nutmeg
1	measuring teaspoon salt
2	cups ripe mashed bananas (4 to 6 medium bananas)
1½	cups sugar
2	eggs
½	cup butter, melted
½	cup milk
2⅔	cups chopped pecans, divided
1	12-ounce package (2 cups) Nestlé Butterscotch Morsels

Preheat oven to 350°F. In a small bowl, combine flour, baking powder, baking soda, cinnamon, nutmeg and salt; set aside. In a large bowl, combine bananas, sugar, eggs and butter; beat until creamy. Gradually add flour mixture alternately with milk; mix until well blended. Stir in 2 cups pecans and the Nestlé Butterscotch Morsels. Pour batter equally into two well-greased and floured 9x5x3-inch loaf pans. Sprinkle tops equally with remaining ⅔ cup pecans. Bake 60 to 70 minutes. Cool 15 minutes; remove from pans.

Makes 2 loaves

Note: To make 1 loaf, divide ingredients in half.

Granola Coffee Ring

CAKE

- 1   **cup granola**
- ¾   **cup sour cream**
- 1   **cup *unsifted* flour**
- ¾   **measuring teaspoon baking soda**
- ¾   **measuring teaspoon baking powder**
- ½   **measuring teaspoon salt**
- ½   **measuring teaspoon mace**
- ½   **cup butter, softened**
- ½   **cup sugar**
- 3   **eggs**

FILLING

- ½   **cup firmly packed brown sugar**
- ½   **cup chopped nuts**
- 2   **measuring tablespoons sour cream**
- ½   **measuring teaspoon cinnamon**
- 1   **6-ounce package (1 cup) Nestlé Butterscotch Morsels**

CAKE: In a large bowl, combine granola and sour cream; let stand 15 minutes to soften cereal. Preheat oven to 350°F. In a small bowl, combine flour, baking soda, baking powder, salt and mace; set aside. Beat butter, sugar and eggs into granola-sour cream mixture. Stir in flour mixture; set aside.

FILLING: In a small bowl, mix brown sugar, nuts, sour cream and cinnamon. Spread half the granola batter into greased and floured 10-inch tube pan; dot with half the filling and sprinkle with Nestlé Butterscotch Morsels. Cover with remaining batter; top with remaining filling. Bake 50 minutes. Loosen edges. Cool cake completely; remove from pan.

Makes one 10-inch coffee cake

Warm up a winter day for good friends: Invite them in for invigorating cupfuls of Rich Hot Chocolate, surprise them with a homemade spice-perfumed granola ring.

Bird's Nest Coffeecake

1	6-ounce package (1 cup) Nestlé Semi-Sweet Real Chocolate Morsels, divided
¼	cup blanched slivered almonds, toasted
1	measuring teaspoon grated orange rind
2¼	to 3¼ cups *unsifted* flour
¼	cup sugar
1	measuring teaspoon salt
1	¼-ounce package dry yeast
⅔	cup milk
2	measuring tablespoons butter
2	eggs
	Melted butter
5	raw eggs in shells, colored with food coloring
1	measuring tablespoon vegetable shortening

In a small bowl, combine ¾ cup Nestlé Semi-Sweet Real Chocolate Morsels, almonds and orange rind; set aside. In a large bowl, combine 1 cup flour, sugar, salt and undissolved yeast; set aside. In a small saucepan, combine milk and butter over low heat until liquid is warm (120 to 130°F.). Gradually add to flour mixture; beat 2 minutes at medium speed with electric mixer. Add 2 eggs and enough flour to make a thick batter. Beat 2 minutes at high speed; stir in enough additional flour to make a soft dough. Gently stir in morsel-almond mixture. Turn onto a lightly floured board; knead until smooth and elastic (about 8 to 10 minutes). Place in lightly greased bowl, turning dough to grease top. Cover; let rise in a warm place until doubled in bulk (about 1 hour).

Punch down dough; turn onto a lightly floured board and divide in half. Roll each half into a 24-inch rope. Place ropes side by side on a lightly greased cookie sheet and loosely overlap one with the other, starting in the middle. Shape into a ring and seal ends. Brush ring with melted butter. Place colored eggs in spaces in the twist. Cover; let rise in a warm place until doubled in bulk (about 1 hour). About 15 to 20 minutes before ready to bake, preheat oven to 350°F. Bake 30 to 35 minutes. Remove from cookie sheet; cool on rack.

Over hot (not boiling) water, heat remaining ¼ cup Nestlé Semi-Sweet Real Chocolate Morsels and the shortening; stir until morsels melt and mixture is smooth. Drizzle chocolate mixture over completely cooled ring to resemble a bird's nest.

Makes one 9-inch coffeecake

Bird's Nest Coffeecake

Pies

Grandma's pies were good and she was proud of them. She was continuing a tradition that began with the Pilgrims. Their pies were simple, hearty fare; Grandma's, too, were delicious concoctions using the fresh fruits of the season.

Today's pies are richer—gossamer chocolate custards topped with clouds of freshly whipped cream or foamy meringue. And so the line continues, with new things building on the old. It's hard to fault a pie with its miracle of lightness and intensity of flavor, the crunchy darkness of a nut-filled chocolate shell contrasting with a froth of taste and color.

Try this collection of ethereal pies created especially for you. They're as pretty to look at as they are delicious to eat.

Pink Peppermint Pie

Pink Peppermint Pie

1   9-inch baked pie shell
1   6-ounce package (1 cup) Nestlé Semi-Sweet Real
    Chocolate Morsels
⅓   cup milk
2½ cups miniature marshmallows
½   cup milk
¼   measuring teaspoon salt
¼   measuring teaspoon peppermint extract
⅛   measuring teaspoon red food coloring
1   cup heavy cream, whipped

Over hot (not boiling) water, combine Nestlé Semi-Sweet Real
Chocolate Morsels and ⅓ cup milk; heat until morsels melt and
mixture is smooth. Remove from heat; set aside. Over hot (not
boiling) water, combine marshmallows, ½ cup milk, the salt, peppermint extract and food coloring; heat, stirring constantly, until
marshmallows melt and mixture is smooth. Transfer to a large
bowl; chill in refrigerator until slightly thickened (about 45 to 60
minutes). Stir until smooth. Gently fold in whipped cream. Spread
half the peppermint mixture into pie shell. Dollop with half the
chocolate mixture. With a knife, swirl chocolate mixture in a figure-
eight pattern. Repeat procedure with remaining peppermint and
chocolate mixtures. Chill until firm (about 2 hours).

Makes one 9-inch pie

Butterscotch Pecan Pie

1   12-ounce package (2 cups) Nestlé Butterscotch Morsels
1   cup dark corn syrup
4   eggs
½   measuring teaspoon salt
1   cup pecan halves
1   9-inch unbaked pie shell
    Whipped cream and pecan halves for garnish (optional)

Preheat oven to 350°F. Melt Nestlé Butterscotch Morsels over hot
(not boiling) water; remove from heat and set aside. In a large bowl,
combine corn syrup, eggs and salt; beat well. Gradually blend in
melted butterscotch, beat until smooth. Stir in pecans. Pour into
unbaked pie shell. Bake 50 minutes. Cool. Garnish with dollops of
whipped cream and pecan halves, if desired.
Makes one 9-inch pie

Chocolate-Coconut Mousse Pie

COCONUT CRUST

- ¼ **cup butter**
- 2 **3⅓-ounce cans (2⅔ cups) shredded coconut**

CHOCOLATE MOUSSE FILLING

- 1 **11½-ounce package (2 cups) Nestlé Milk Chocolate Morsels**
- ¼ **pound (16 large) marshmallows**
- ½ **cup milk**
- ⅛ **measuring teaspoon salt**
- 1 **cup heavy cream**

COCONUT CRUST: Melt butter in a large skillet. Add coconut; stir occasionally until lightly toasted. Press evenly on bottom and side (not over rim) of buttered 9-inch pie pan. Chill in refrigerator 30 minutes.

CHOCOLATE MOUSSE FILLING: Over hot (not boiling) water, combine Nestlé Milk Chocolate Morsels, marshmallows, milk and salt; heat until morsels and marshmallows melt and mixture is smooth. Cool mixture thoroughly in refrigerator (1 to 1½ hours).

In a small bowl, beat heavy cream until stiff peaks form. Fold into cooled chocolate mixture. Pour into prepared Coconut Crust. Chill in refrigerator at least 2 hours before serving.

Makes one 9-inch pie

Heavenly Cream Cheese Pie

CHOCOLATE NUT CRUST

- 1   6-ounce package (1 cup) Nestlé Semi-Sweet Real Chocolate Morsels
- 1   measuring tablespoon vegetable shortening
- 1½   cups finely chopped nuts

FILLING

- 1   6-ounce package (1 cup) Nestlé Semi-Sweet Real Chocolate Morsels
- 1   8-ounce package cream cheese, softened
- ¾   cup sugar, divided
- ⅛   measuring teaspoon salt
- 2   eggs, separated
- 1   cup heavy cream
- 3   measuring tablespoons brandy
  Whipped cream for garnish (optional)

CHOCOLATE NUT CRUST: Line a 9-inch pie pan with foil. Over hot (not boiling) water, melt Nestlé Semi-Sweet Real Chocolate Morsels and shortening; stir in nuts. Spread evenly on bottom and side (not over rim) of prepared pie pan. Chill in refrigerator until firm (about 1 hour). Lift out of pan; peel off foil. Replace crust in pan; chill until ready to fill.

FILLING: Melt Nestlé Semi-Sweet Real Chocolate Morsels over hot (not boiling) water; cool 10 minutes. In a large bowl, combine cream cheese, ½ cup sugar and the salt; beat until creamy. Beat in egg yolks, one at a time. Stir in cooled chocolate; set aside. In a small bowl, beat egg whites until foamy. Gradually add ¼ cup sugar and beat until stiff, glossy peaks form. Set aside. In a small bowl, beat heavy cream and brandy until stiff peaks form. Fold whipped cream and beaten egg whites into chocolate mixture. Pour into Chocolate Nut Crust. Chill in refrigerator until firm (about 3 hours). Garnish with whipped cream, if desired.

Makes one 9-inch pie

Grasshopper Pie

CHOCO-NUT CRUST

1 6-ounce package (1 cup) Nestlé Semi-Sweet Real Chocolate Morsels
1 measuring tablespoon vegetable shortening
1½ cups finely chopped nuts

FILLING

½ pound marshmallows (about 40 large)
⅓ cup milk
¼ measuring teaspoon salt
3 measuring tablespoons green crème de menthe
3 measuring tablespoons white crème de cacao
1½ cups heavy cream, whipped

CHOCO-NUT CRUST: Line a 9-inch pie pan with foil. Over hot (not boiling) water, melt Nestlé Semi-Sweet Real Chocolate Morsels and shortening. Add chopped nuts; mix well. Spread evenly on bottom and side (not over rim) of prepared pie pan. Chill in refrigerator until firm (about 1 hour). Lift shell out of pan; peel off foil. Replace shell in pan or place on serving plate; chill in refrigerator.

FILLING: Over hot (not boiling) water, combine marshmallows, milk and salt; heat until marshmallows melt. Remove from heat. Add liqueurs; stir until blended. Chill in refrigerator, stirring occasionally, until slightly thickened (about 30 to 45 minutes). Gently fold in whipped cream. Pour half the filling into prepared Choco-Nut Crust; spoon on remaining filling, forming a design. Garnish with Chocolate Curls (page 133), if desired. Chill until firm (about 1 hour).

Makes one 9-inch pie

FLAVOR VARIATIONS: *Substitute the following for the crème de menthe and crème de cacao. Garnish as indicated.*

Substitute: *3 measuring tablespoons almond liqueur.* **Garnish:** *Toasted slivered almonds.*

Substitute: *¼ cup coffee liqueur and ¼ cup vodka.* **Garnish:** *Chopped Nestlé Semi-Sweet Real Chocolate Morsels.*

Substitute: *3 measuring tablespoons orange liqueur; 1 measuring teaspoon grated orange rind.* **Garnish:** *Orange rind slivers.*

*Grasshopper Pie; Grasshopper Tarts filled with
orange liqueur and coffee liqueur flavor variations*

Grasshopper Tarts

1   **6-ounce package (1 cup) Nestlé Semi-Sweet Real Chocolate Morsels**
1   **measuring tablespoon vegetable shortening**
1½   **cups finely chopped nuts**
     Grasshopper Pie filling or flavor variation (page 94)

Line 10 tart or muffin cups with foil. Over hot (not boiling) water, melt Nestlé Semi-Sweet Real Chocolate Morsels and shortening. Add chopped nuts; mix well. Spoon 2 measuring tablespoons mixture into prepared cups; spread evenly on bottom and up sides, using a spatula or spoon. Chill in refrigerator until firm (about 1 hour). Peel foil liners from chocolate cups. Place on serving plate. Using a pastry bag fitted with a decorative tip, pipe Grasshopper Pie filling (or flavor variation) into each chocolate cup. Chill until firm (about 1 hour).

Makes 10 tarts

Chocolate Cream Pie

1   **11½-ounce package (1 cup) Nestle Milk Chocolate Morsels, divided**
1   **measuring tablespoon vegetable shortening**
1½   **cups finely chopped nuts**
1   **3¾-ounce package vanilla *instant* pudding and pie filling**
1   **cup sour cream**
1   **cup milk**
1   **cup heavy cream, sweetened and whipped**

CHOCOLATE SHELL: Line a 9-inch pie pan with foil. Over hot (not boiling) water, melt 1 cup Nestlé Milk Chocolate Morsels and the shortening; stir in nuts. Spread evenly on bottom and side (not over rim of prepared pie pan. Chill until firm (about 1 hour). Lift shell out of pan; peel off foil. Replace shell in pan; chill.

FILLING: Melt 1 cup Nestlé Milk Chocolate Morsels over hot (not boiling) water. Remove from heat; set aside. In a small bowl, combine instant pudding powder, sour cream and milk; mix well. Beat in melted chocolate. Pour into prepared Chocolate Shell. Chill in refrigerator about 2 hours. Before serving, garnish top with sweetened whipped cream.

Makes one 9-inch pie

Chocolate-Rum Striped Pie

1   12-ounce package (2 cups) Nestlé Semi-Sweet Real
    Chocolate Morsels
1   cup milk
¼   cup sugar
1   envelope (1 measuring tablespoon) unflavored gelatin
½   measuring teaspoon salt
2   eggs, separated
¼   cup rum
½   cup sugar
1   cup heavy cream
2   measuring tablespoons confectioners' sugar
1   9-inch baked pie shell

Over hot (not boiling) water, combine Nestlé Semi-Sweet Real
Chocolate Morsels, milk, ¼ cup sugar, gelatin and salt; heat until
gelatin is dissolved and mixture is smooth. Quickly beat in egg yolks
and continue cooking for 2 minutes, stirring constantly. Remove
from heat; stir in rum. Chill in refrigerator until completely cool and
slightly thickened (about 1 hour).

In a small bowl, beat egg whites until frothy. Gradually beat in ½
cup sugar and continue beating until stiff, glossy peaks form. Fold
into cooled chocolate mixture; set aside. In a small bowl, combine
cream and confectioners' sugar; beat until stiff peaks form. Spread
half the chocolate mixture into pie shell. Spread 1¼ cups whipped
cream over chocolate layer. Cover with remaining chocolate mixture. Decorate top with dollops of remaining whipped cream or
pipe through pastry tube. Chill pie in refrigerator until firm
(about 1 hour).

Makes one 9-inch pie

Black Bottom Pie

1   cup sugar, divided
¼   cup cornstarch
2   cups milk, scalded
3   eggs, separated
1   6-ounce package (1 cup) Nestlé Semi-Sweet Real
     Chocolate Morsels
2½   measuring tablespoons vanilla extract, divided
1   9-inch baked pie shell
¼   cup cold water
1   envelope (1 measuring tablespoon) unflavored gelatin
¼   measuring teaspoon cream of tartar
½   cup heavy cream, whipped
     Chocolate shavings (optional)

CHOCOLATE LAYER: In a large saucepan, combine ½ cup sugar and the cornstarch; mix well. Gradually stir in scalded milk. Add some of the hot milk mixture to the egg yolks; mix well. Return to remaining milk mixture. Cook over moderate heat, stirring constantly, until mixture thickens (about 5 minutes). Remove 1 cup hot milk mixture to a small bowl; add Nestlé Semi-Sweet Real Chocolate Morsels and 1½ measuring teaspoons vanilla extract. Stir until morsels melt and mixture is smooth. Pour into prepared pie shell; set aside.

VANILLA LAYER: In a large bowl, combine cold water, gelatin and 2 measuring tablespoons vanilla extract; let stand 5 minutes. Add remaining hot milk mixture from saucepan; stir until gelatin dissolves. Cool 15 minutes at room temperature. Cover surface with plastic wrap or waxed paper. In a small bowl, combine egg whites and cream of tartar; beat until foamy. Gradually add ½ cup sugar; beat until stiff peaks form. Fold into cooled gelatin mixture along with whipped cream. Pour over chocolate layer. Chill in refrigerator until set (about 2 hours). Garnish top of pie with chocolate shavings, if desired.

Makes one 9-inch pie

Chocolate-Almond Pie

1   6-ounce package (1 cup) Nestlé Semi-Sweet Real
       Chocolate Morsels
1   cup light corn syrup
3   eggs
⅓   cup sugar
¼   cup butter, melted
½   measuring teaspoon salt
1   cup coarsely chopped almonds, toasted
1   9-inch unbaked pie shell
    Whipped cream and whole almonds for garnish (optional)

Preheat oven to 375°F. Melt Nestlé Semi-Sweet Real Chocolate
Morsels over hot (not boiling) water; remove from heat and cool at
room temperature 5 minutes. In a large bowl, combine corn syrup,
eggs, sugar, butter and salt; beat well. Gradually blend in melted
chocolate; beat until smooth. Stir in chopped almonds. Pour into
unbaked pie shell. Bake 45 to 50 minutes. Cool. Garnish with dollops of whipped cream and whole almonds, if desired.

Makes one 9-inch pie

Chocolate Fudge Cheese Pie

1   6-ounce package (1 cup) Nestlé Semi-Sweet Real
       Chocolate Morsels
¼   cup milk
1   8-ounce package cream cheese, softened
1   cup sugar
1   measuring teaspoon vanilla extract
¼   measuring teaspoon salt
3   eggs
1   9-inch graham cracker crust
¼   cup chopped nuts

Preheat oven to 325°F. Over hot (not boiling) water, combine
Nestlé Semi-Sweet Real Chocolate Morsels and milk; stir until morsels melt and mixture is smooth. Remove from heat and set aside.
In a large bowl, combine cream cheese, sugar, vanilla extract and
salt; beat until creamy. Add eggs, one at a time, beating well after
each addition. Blend in chocolate mixture. Pour into pie crust.
Sprinkle top with nuts. Bake 50 minutes.

Makes one 9-inch pie

Pumpkin Chiffon Pie

CHOCO-WALNUT CRUST

- **1** **6-ounce package (1 cup) Nestlé Semi-Sweet Real Chocolate Morsels**
- **2** **measuring tablespoons vegetable shortening**
- **1** **cup finely chopped walnuts**

PUMPKIN CHIFFON FILLING

- **¾** **cup sugar, divided**
- **1** **envelope (1 measuring tablespoon) unflavored gelatin**
- **½** **measuring teaspoon salt**
- **½** **measuring teaspoon cinnamon**
- **¼** **measuring teaspoon nutmeg**
- **¾** **cup milk**
- **2** **eggs, separated**
- **1** **cup canned pumpkin**
- **1** **measuring teaspoon vanilla extract**
- **½** **cup heavy cream, whipped**

CHOCO-WALNUT CRUST: Line a 9-inch pie pan with foil. Over hot (not boiling) water, melt Nestlé Semi-Sweet Real Chocolate Morsels and shortening; stir in walnuts. Spread evenly on bottom and side (not over rim) of prepared pie pan. Chill in refrigerator until firm (about 1 hour). Lift out of pan; peel off foil. Replace shell in pan; chill in refrigerator until ready to fill.

PUMPKIN CHIFFON FILLING: In a large saucepan, combine ½ cup sugar, the gelatin, salt, cinnamon and nutmeg. Stir in milk, egg yolks and pumpkin. Cook over medium heat until mixture boils and gelatin dissolves. Remove from heat; add vanilla extract. Transfer mixture to a small bowl. Set bowl over an ice bath; chill until mixture mounds from a spoon (about 30 minutes). In a small bowl, beat egg whites until soft peaks form. Gradually add remaining ¼ cup sugar and beat until stiff peaks form. Fold into pumpkin mixture alternately with whipped cream. Pour into prepared Choco-Walnut Crust. Chill until firm (about 1 hour).

Makes one 9-inch pie

"Said old Gentleman Gay, 'On a Thanksgiving Day,
If you want a good time, then give something away.'"

—Marion Douglas, A Good Thanksgiving

From top: Pumpkin Chiffon Pie,
Chocolate-Coconut Mousse Pie

Chilled and Frozen Desserts

It used to be, half a century or more ago, the children who prepared dessert for summer Sunday dinners. Squatting in the sun-dappled shade, they smashed hunks of ice in burlap bags with wooden mallets. Once the precious cylinder containing the cream was inserted in the wooden bucket, they surrounded it with crushed ice and rock salt and, amidst amiable bickering, took turns cranking until the handle would move no more. It was hot work, but at the end there was the prize—the dasher to lick, with each helper getting a share. And the family was provided with a lavish dessert, cool perfection to wind up a summer meal.

The air of timeless leisure created by those luscious ice-cream desserts can be recaptured in the recipes in this chapter. They will get you down to the chocolate heart of matters with an array as dazzling to the eye as tempting to the taste. Cooling in the summer and soothing after elaborate dinners, they will shine as the crown jewels of your well-set table.

Chocolate-Mint Soufflé

1   6-ounce package (1 cup) Nestlé Semi-Sweet Real
    Chocolate Morsels
1   envelope (1 measuring tablespoon) unflavored gelatin
1   cup sugar, divided
6   eggs, separated
½   cup milk
¼   cup water
1   measuring teaspoon peppermint extract
    Green food coloring
¼   measuring teaspoon salt
1   cup heavy cream, whipped

Prepare a 2-inch foil collar for a 1¼- to 1½-quart soufflé dish. Lightly oil collar and fasten to dish; set aside. In blender container, process Nestlé Semi-Sweet Real Chocolate Morsels at high speed about 15 seconds or until reduced to fine particles; set aside, reserving 1 measuring tablespoon for garnish. In a large saucepan, combine gelatin and ½ cup sugar; set aside. In a small bowl, beat egg yolks with milk and water; blend into gelatin mixture. Cook over moderate heat, stirring constantly with a wire whisk, until gelatin is completely dissolved, and mixture thickens slightly and coats a spoon (about 8 to 10 minutes). Stir in peppermint extract and food coloring. Cool at room temperature 15 to 20 minutes, stirring occasionally (mixture will be lukewarm).

In a large bowl, beat egg whites and salt until soft peaks form. Gradually beat in remaining ½ cup sugar until stiff peaks form; set aside. Gently fold peppermint-egg yolk mixture, whipped cream and ground chocolate into egg whites. Turn into prepared soufflé dish. Sprinkle top with reserved morsels. Chill in refrigerator until firm (about 4 to 5 hours). Remove collar before serving.

Makes 6 to 8 servings

MOCHA SOUFFLÉ: *Omit peppermint extract and green food coloring. Add 2 measuring tablespoons instant coffee to combined gelatin and sugar.*

Chocolate-Mint Soufflé

105

Minted Pears with Chocolate Sauce

MINTED PEARS

8   pears
1½   cups water
1   cup white crème de menthe
1   cup sugar

CHOCOLATE SAUCE

¾   cup sweetened condensed milk*
¼   cup water
1   measuring tablespoon butter
¼   measuring teaspoon salt
1   6-ounce package (1 cup) Nestlé Semi-Sweet Real
      Chocolate Morsels
1   measuring teaspoon vanilla extract

MINTED PEARS: Core pears from bottom. If possible, leave stem in. Remove peel from top half of pear, forming a decorative scalloped bottom with remaining peel. In a 4-quart Dutch oven or large saucepot, combine water, crème de menthe and sugar; bring to a boil. Add pears; cover and simmer 5 to 10 minutes until tender. Remove from heat and cool at room temperature (about 30 minutes). Chill in refrigerator (about 1 hour). When ready to serve, spoon about 3 measuring tablespoons Chocolate Sauce (below) over each pear.

CHOCOLATE SAUCE: In a large saucepan, combine sweetened condensed milk, water, butter and salt; *bring to full boil* over medium heat. *Boil 1 minute,* stirring constantly, over medium heat. Remove from heat. Add Nestlé Semi-Sweet Real Chocolate Morsels and vanilla extract; stir until mixture is smooth.

Makes 8 servings

*Not evaporated milk

Chocolate-Orange Puffs

ORANGE PUFFS

- ½ **cup water**
- ¼ **cup butter**
- 1 **measuring tablespoon grated orange rind**
  Dash salt
- ½ **cup** *unsifted* **flour**
- 2 **eggs**
  Confectioners' sugar

CHOCOLATE FILLING

- 1 **6-ounce package (1 cup) Nestlé Semi-Sweet Real Chocolate Morsels**
- 3 **measuring tablespoons orange juice**
- ⅔ **cup heavy cream**
- 3 **measuring tablespoons confectioners' sugar**
  Dash salt

ORANGE PUFFS: Preheat oven to 450°F. In a small saucepan, combine water, butter, orange rind and salt; heat until mixture boils. Remove from heat. Add flour; blend until mixture holds together. Add eggs, one at a time, beating well after each addition. Drop dough by level measuring tablespoonfuls onto ungreased cookie sheets. Bake 10 minutes. Reduce heat to 350° F.; bake 10 minutes longer. Remove from oven. While still hot, cut a thin slice from top of each puff. Cool completely. Spoon about 1 rounded measuring tablespoonful Chocolate Filling (below) into each puff. Replace top. Dust top with confectioners' sugar. Chill in refrigerator about 1 hour or until ready to serve.

CHOCOLATE FILLING: Over hot (not boiling) water, combine Nestlé Semi-Sweet Real Chocolate Morsels and orange juice; stir until morsels melt and mixture is smooth. Transfer to a large bowl; cool 10 minutes. In a small bowl, combine heavy cream, confectioners' sugar and salt; beat until stiff peaks form. Gently fold into cooled chocolate mixture.

Makes 16 puffs

Chocolate Bavarian

Chocolate Bavarian

2   envelopes (2 measuring tablespoons) unflavored gelatin
1   cup sugar, divided
¼   measuring teaspoon salt
4   eggs, separated
2   cups milk
1   12-ounce package (2 cups) Nestlé Semi-Sweet Real
    Chocolate Morsels
2   measuring teaspoons vanilla extract
2   cups heavy cream, whipped
    Whipped cream for garnish (optional)
    Chocolate Curls, page 133 (optional)

In a large saucepan, combine gelatin, ½ cup sugar and the salt. In a small bowl, beat egg yolks and milk; stir into gelatin mixture. Add Nestlé Semi-Sweet Real Chocolate Morsels and cook over medium heat, stirring constantly, until morsels are melted and gelatin is dissolved (about 8 minutes). Remove from heat and stir in vanilla extract. Chill, stirring occasionally, until mixture mounds when dropped from a spoon. In a small bowl, beat egg whites until stiff but not dry. Gradually add remaining ½ cup sugar, beating until very stiff. Fold in chilled chocolate mixture alternately with whipped cream. Turn into 8-cup decorative mold. Chill in refrigerator until firm. Unmold onto a serving platter. Garnish with whipped cream and/or Chocolate Curls, if desired.

Makes 12 servings

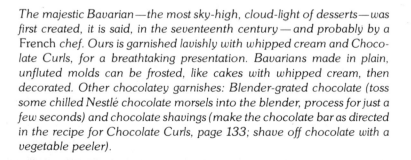

The majestic Bavarian—the most sky-high, cloud-light of desserts—was first created, it is said, in the seventeenth century—and probably by a French chef. Ours is garnished lavishly with whipped cream and Chocolate Curls, for a breathtaking presentation. Bavarians made in plain, unfluted molds can be frosted, like cakes with whipped cream, then decorated. Other chocolatey garnishes: Blender-grated chocolate (toss some chilled Nestlé chocolate morsels into the blender, process for just a few seconds) and chocolate shavings (make the chocolate bar as directed in the recipe for Chocolate Curls, page 133; shave off chocolate with a vegetable peeler).

Blender Pots de Crème

1 12-ounce package (2 cups) Nestlé Semi-Sweet Real
   Chocolate Morsels
½ cup sugar
3 eggs
1 cup hot milk
2 to 4 measuring tablespoons brandy, rum, or almond or
   orange liqueurs
   Whipped cream (optional)

In blender container, combine Nestlé Semi-Sweet Real Chocolate Morsels, sugar and eggs. Add hot milk and liquor; blend at medium speed until mixture is smooth. Pour into pots de crème or demitasse cups and chill in refrigerator 1 hour. Garnish with whipped cream, if desired. *Keep in refrigerator* until ready to serve.

Makes 8 4-ounce servings

MOCHA MOUSSE: Add 3 measuring tablespoons instant coffee to blender along with eggs.

Chocolate Mousse

1 6-ounce package (1 cup) Nestlé Semi-Sweet Real
   Chocolate Morsels
3 eggs, separated
¼ cup water
⅛ teaspoon salt
⅓ cup firmly packed brown sugar

Melt Nestlé Semi-Sweet Real Chocolate Morsels over hot (not boiling) water; remove from heat. Add egg yolks, one at a time, beating well after each addition. Add water; beat until smooth. In a small bowl, combine egg whites and salt; beat until soft peaks form. Gradually beat in brown sugar and continue beating until stiff, glossy peaks form. Gently fold in chocolate mixture. Chill in refrigerator several hours or until ready to serve.

Makes 4 to 6 servings

Note: Because it contains raw eggs, be sure to keep mousse refrigerated.

Pots de Crème, Butterscotch Thins

Chocolate Cups

1   6-ounce package (1 cup) Nestlé Semi-Sweet Real
    Chocolate Morsels
1   measuring tablespoon vegetable shortening
9   foil cupcake liners

Over hot (not boiling) water, combine Nestlé Semi-Sweet Real
Chocolate Morsels and vegetable shortening; heat until morsels
melt and mixture is smooth. Coat inside of each cupcake liner with
1 measuring tablespoon chocolate mixture. Place cupcake liner in
palm of hand; rotate gently, using rubber spatula to push chocolate
up sides. Place coated liners in muffin pans. Chill in refrigerator
until firm (about 1 hour). Lift liners from muffin pans; peel foil off
shells. Return chocolate shells to pan. Chill until ready to use. Fill
with cold or frozen fillings such as pudding, custard, mousse or
ice cream.

Makes 9 chocolate cups

Note: For 24 miniature cups, use gem-size foil liners and gem pan.

Party Parfaits

1   6-ounce package (1 cup) Nestlé Semi-Sweet Real
    Chocolate Morsels
1   6-ounce package (1 cup) Nestlé Butterscotch Morsels
2   3¾-ounce packages vanilla *instant* pudding and
    pie filling
2   cups milk
2   cups sour cream

Melt Nestlé Semi-Sweet Real Chocolate Morsels over hot (not boiling) water; remove from heat and set aside. Repeat with Nestlé
Butterscotch Morsels. In a large bowl, combine instant pudding
powder, milk and sour cream. Mix pudding according to package
directions. Transfer half the pudding to a small bowl; using a wire
whisk or electric beater, blend in the melted chocolate. Repeat with
remaining pudding, using melted butterscotch. Spoon about 2
rounded measuring tablespoonfuls chocolate mixture alternately
with equal amount butterscotch mixture into each of five 7-ounce
parfait glasses. Chill in refrigerator until ready to serve.

Makes 5 servings

Quick Napoleons

2   cups milk
1   3¾-ounce package vanilla *instant* pudding and pie filling
1   cup heavy cream
1   6-ounce package (1 cup) Nestlé Semi-Sweet Real
     Chocolate Morsels
24 cinnamon graham crackers
1½ cups sifted confectioners' sugar
2   measuring tablespoons milk
1   measuring teaspoon corn syrup

Using 2 cups milk, prepare instant pudding according to package directions. In a small bowl, beat heavy cream until stiff; fold into prepared pudding and chill in refrigerator. Melt Nestlé Semi-Sweet Real Chocolate Morsels over hot (not boiling) water. Spread each of 16 crackers with 1 teaspoon melted chocolate. Reserve remaining melted chocolate for frosting. Line a 13x9x2-inch pan with foil and arrange 8 chocolate-covered crackers on bottom. Carefully spread half the chilled pudding mixture evenly over crackers. Repeat with a layer of 8 chocolate-covered crackers and remaining pudding. Set aside; prepare frosting.

In a small bowl, combine confectioners' sugar, 2 measuring tablespoons milk and the corn syrup; blend well. Prepare remaining crackers, one at a time: Spread crackers with confectioners' sugar glaze. Fit a pastry tube with a writing tip and fill with remaining melted chocolate. For a "feathered" look, pipe chocolate over glaze in lengthwise lines about 1 inch apart. Draw a toothpick or knife point through lines, crosswise, in alternating directions, about 1 inch apart. Place frosted graham crackers on top of final pudding layer. Chill overnight. If desired, cut each napoleon in thirds.

Makes 24 napoleons

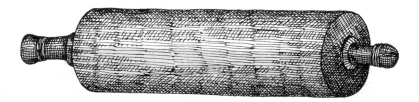

Chocolate-Raspberry Trifle

Chocolate-Raspberry Trifle

1   3-ounce package ladyfingers
¼   cup rum (optional)
½   cup raspberry preserves
1   6-ounce package (1 cup) Nestlé Semi-Sweet Real
    Chocolate Morsels
1   cup milk
1   cup sour cream
1   3¾-ounce package vanilla *instant* pudding and pie filling
1   cup heavy cream
1   measuring tablespoon confectioners' sugar

Arrange ladyfingers on bottom and up sides of a 2½-quart glass bowl. Pour rum evenly over ladyfingers. Spread preserves over ladyfingers. Cover dish with foil and chill in refrigerator about 2 hours.

Melt Nestlé Semi-Sweet Real Chocolate Morsels over hot (not boiling) water. Remove from heat and cool 5 minutes. In a small bowl, combine milk, sour cream and instant pudding powder; beat until thick and creamy. Fold in melted chocolate; spoon carefully into ladyfinger-lined bowl. Chill in refrigerator at least 30 minutes.

In a small bowl, combine heavy cream and confectioners' sugar; beat until stiff. Decorate top of trifle with dollops of whipped cream or pipe through a pastry tube. Refrigerate until ready to serve.

Makes 6 to 8 servings

Duffs and buckles; slumps and grunts; flummeries and fools. Like the titles of folk melodies, the euphonious names of the fruit pudding-desserts of England and Colonial America have been passed down through generations. (And who doesn't know that apple pandowdy is... naturally... a dowdy made in a pan?) "Trifle" may seem a misnomer for a dessert of such heady richness as this: the appellation actually embraces a family of concoctions that traditionally combine custard, fruits, spongecake slices or macaroons, and spiritous liquors (the last ingredient a reminder of the dessert's other soubriquet: tipsy cake). A standard offering on holiday tables in England, a cool, refreshing trifle is equally irresistible on a midsummer table.

Butterscotch Mandarin Trifle

TRIFLE

- 1   3-ounce package ladyfingers
- ¼ cup orange juice
- 1   6-ounce package (1 cup) Nestlé Butterscotch Morsels
- 1   cup milk
- 1   cup sour cream
- 1   3¾-ounce package vanilla *instant* pudding and pie filling
- ½ measuring teaspoon orange extract
- 1   11-ounce can mandarin oranges, drained

GARNISH

- 1   cup heavy cream
- 1   measuring tablespoon confectioners' sugar
- ¼ cup pecan halves

TRIFLE: Arrange ladyfingers on bottom and up sides of a 2½-quart glass bowl. Brush orange juice evenly over ladyfingers. Cover dish with foil and chill in refrigerator about 2 hours.

Melt Nestlé Butterscotch Morsels over hot (not boiling) water. Remove from heat and cool 5 minutes. In a large bowl, combine milk, sour cream, instant pudding powder and orange extract; beat until thick and creamy. Gradually beat in melted butterscotch; set aside. Spoon oranges over ladyfingers. Spoon butterscotch pudding mixture over oranges; cover and chill in refrigerator at least 30 minutes. Decorate with garnish (below); refrigerate until ready to serve.

GARNISH: In a small bowl, combine heavy cream and confectioners' sugar; beat until stiff peaks form. Decorate top of trifle with dollops of whipped cream or pipe through a pastry tube. Garnish whipped cream with pecan halves.

Makes 6 to 8 servings

"A trifle can be a pretty thing, and it needs a pretty dish..."

—M. F. K. Fisher

Chocolate Floating Islands

½ **cup sugar**
3 **measuring tablespoons cornstarch**
½ **measuring teaspoon salt**
2 **cups milk**
1 **egg**
1 **egg, separated**
1 **6-ounce package (1 cup) Nestlé Semi-Sweet Real
   Chocolate Morsels**
1 **measuring teaspoon vanilla extract**
2 **measuring tablespoons sugar**

In a small saucepan, combine ½ cup sugar, the cornstarch and salt; stir to blend. Gradually add milk, stirring constantly until smooth. Cook over high heat, stirring constantly, until mixture thickens (about 3 to 5 minutes). In a small bowl, beat whole egg and egg yolk slightly. Stir in some of the hot milk mixture; mix well, then quickly transfer to remaining hot mixture. Remove from heat. Add Nestlé Semi-Sweet Real Chocolate Morsels and vanilla extract; stir until melted and smooth. Cool at room temperature about 5 minutes, then spoon into dessert dishes. Chill in refrigerator at least 1½ hours or until ready to serve.

In a small bowl, beat egg white until soft peaks form. Gradually add 2 measuring tablespoons sugar and beat until stiff but not dry. In a shallow pan, bring water (¼ inch deep) to a simmer. Drop meringue by heaping tablespoonfuls into simmering water. Simmer uncovered over medium heat about 5 minutes. Lift meringues from water with a slotted spoon; drain on paper towels. Place on top of chilled chocolate custard.

Makes 5 ½-cup servings

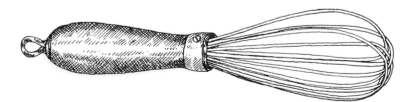

Frozen Mocha Charlotte

2	measuring teaspoons butter, softened
2	measuring tablespoons sugar
2	3-ounce packages ladyfingers
¼	cup light rum
1	12-ounce package (2 cups) Nestlé Semi-Sweet Real Chocolate Morsels
3	measuring tablespoons instant coffee
½	cup boiling water
6	eggs, separated
½	cup sugar
½	measuring teaspoon vanilla extract
¼	measuring teaspoon coconut extract
2	cups heavy cream, whipped
¼	cup ground nuts

Butter a 9-inch round springform pan. Sprinkle with 2 tablespoons sugar; set aside. Split ladyfingers (do not separate); brush inside surface with rum. Line side of prepared springform pan with ladyfingers, rounded sides against pan. Separate remaining ladyfingers and line bottom of pan to fit. Melt Nestlé Semi-Sweet Real Chocolate Morsels over hot (not boiling) water; set aside. In a small measuring cup, combine instant coffee and boiling water; stir until dissolved. Set aside. In a large bowl, beat egg yolks until foamy. Gradually beat in ½ cup sugar at high speed until thick and lemon colored (about 4 minutes). Beat in melted chocolate, coffee mixture, and vanilla and coconut extracts; set aside. In a large bowl, beat egg whites until stiff. Fold egg whites and 3 cups of the whipped cream into chocolate mixture. Pour into ladyfinger-lined pan. Freeze until firm (about 2 hours). Pipe rosettes with remaining whipped cream and sprinkle with ground nuts. Allow charlotte to thaw one hour at room temperature before serving. Remove springform ring before serving. Refrigerate any leftover charlotte.

Makes 10 to 12 servings

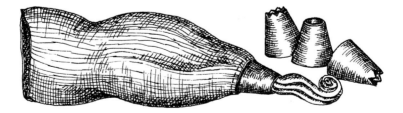

Blender Chocolate Ice Cream

- ½ cup sugar
- ½ cup water
- 1 6-ounce package (1 cup) Nestlé Semi-Sweet Real Chocolate Morsels
- 2 eggs
- 2 measuring teaspoons vanilla extract
- ½ measuring teaspoon salt
- 1½ cups heavy cream, whipped

In a small saucepan, combine sugar and water. Bring to a boil over moderate heat; boil 3 minutes, then remove from heat. In blender container, combine Nestlé Semi-Sweet Real Chocolate Morsels and hot syrup mixture; process at high speed about 6 seconds. Add eggs, vanilla extract and salt; blend for about 1 minute. Pour over whipped cream and mix well. Pour into 9x5x3-inch loaf pan. Freeze until firm.

Makes 1 quart ice cream

Chocolate Dessert Waffles

- 1½ cups milk
- 1 cup sugar
- 3 envelopes (3 ounces) Nestlé Choco-bake
- 1 egg
- 2 measuring tablespoons vegetable oil
- ¾ measuring teaspoon vanilla extract
- ¾ measuring teaspoon cinnamon
- 2 cups buttermilk pancake mix
  Ice cream
  Chocolate sauce

In blender container or a large bowl, combine milk, sugar, Nestlé Choco-bake, egg, oil, vanilla extract and cinnamon; process at medium speed about 10 seconds or beat well. Add pancake mix; blend until smooth (about 1 minute), scraping sides of container if necessary. To bake waffles, follow manufacturer's instructions on waffle iron. Serve with ice cream and chocolate sauce.

Makes 20 3x5-inch waffles

Valentine Ice Cream Torte

120

Valentine Ice Cream Torte

1	12-ounce package (2 cups) Nestlé Semi-Sweet Real Chocolate Morsels, divided
2	3½-ounce cans (2⅔ cups) flaked coconut, divided
2	cups chopped pecans, divided
½	cup plus 2 measuring tablespoons vegetable shortening, melted, divided
2	quarts strawberry ice cream, softened
1	quart chocolate ice cream, softened

In blender container, process ½ cup Nestlé Semi-Sweet Real Chocolate Morsels at high speed about 10 seconds or until reduced to fine particles. In a small bowl, combine ground chocolate, ¼ cup of the coconut, ¼ cup of the pecans and 2 measuring tablespoons melted shortening; mix well. Reserve for garnish. Over hot (not boiling) water, combine remaining 1½ cups Nestlé Semi-Sweet Real Chocolate Morsels and remaining melted shortening; stir until morsels melt and mixture is smooth. Remove from heat but keep mixture over hot water. Stir in remaining coconut and pecans.

Sprinkle about a third of the melted mixture evenly over bottom of 9x3-inch springform pan; press firmly. Chill in freezer until firm, about 5 minutes. Spread 1 quart strawberry ice cream evenly over chocolate mixture; chill in freezer about 10 minutes. Repeat chocolate-nut layer on top of strawberry ice cream; chill in freezer 5 minutes. Spread 1 quart chocolate ice cream evenly over second chocolate-nut layer. Form third and final chocolate-nut layer over chocolate ice cream. Top with remaining quart of strawberry ice cream. Chill in freezer about 10 minutes.

On top of strawberry layer, place a large heart-shaped cookie cutter (open type, without handle); press in about ¼ cup reserved grated chocolate mixture. Remove cookie cutter. Press remaining mixture around top edge of torte to form a decorative edge. Cover pan with plastic wrap or foil and return to freezer until firm, at least 3 hours.

To serve, dip a knife or metal spatula in hot water; run around edge of pan to loosen ice cream. Remove sides of pan. Let torte stand at room temperature 15 to 20 minutes before cutting.

Makes 16 servings

Note: When warm chocolate mixture is spread between layers, ice cream will melt somewhat and seep through.

Special Occasion Desserts

Traditions enrich life, stitching texture into its fabric. Whether it be the annual gathering of friends and family to celebrate the holidays, the remembrance of a birthday or anniversary or the celebration of some other occasion, your family expresses itself in its own special ways.

Food forms the background of these celebrations. The rite of preparing the Christmas fruitcakes takes on a significance of its own. The special huge mixing bowl used but once a year, the nuts and candied fruits to chop, the rich cakes to wrap as gifts and the large cake for the family celebration—all become symbols of your love and concern.

Because we realize the importance of this symbolism, we created some special desserts tailored for special occasions. We know you'll soon find them part of your family tradition, a tradition that will be carried on.

Chocolate Soufflé

Butter
2 **measuring tablespoons graham cracker crumbs**
3 **measuring tablespoons butter**
3 **measuring tablespoons flour**
1 **cup milk**
1 **6-ounce package (1 cup) Nestlé Semi-Sweet Real**
   Chocolate Morsels
4 **eggs, separated**
¼ **cup rum**
1 **measuring teaspoon vanilla extract**
   Vanilla ice cream or sweetened whipped cream

Butter bottom and sides of a 6-cup soufflé dish; coat with graham cracker crumbs. In a small saucepan, melt 3 measuring tablespoons butter over medium heat. Blend in flour. Gradually stir in milk. Cook, stirring constantly, until mixture thickens. Stir in Nestlé Semi-Sweet Real Chocolate Morsels. Transfer chocolate mixture to a large bowl; cool 10 minutes. Beat in egg yolks, rum and vanilla extract; set aside.

Preheat over to 350°F. In a small bowl, beat egg whites until stiff (not dry) peaks form. Stir ½ cup beaten egg whites into chocolate mixture. Gently fold remaining egg whites into chocolate mixture. Pour into prepared dish. For a top-hat soufflé, run knife through batter in a circle 1 inch from edge of dish, to a depth of 1 inch. Bake 40 minutes. Serve immediately with vanilla ice cream or sweetened whipped cream.

Makes 6 to 8 servings

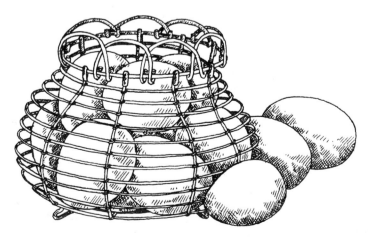

Butterscotch-Nut Crêpes

CRÊPES

1¼ cups milk
1 cup buttermilk pancake mix
1 egg
1 measuring tablespoon vegetable oil
2 measuring tablespoons butter, melted

BUTTERSCOTCH-NUT FILLING

1 6-ounce package (1 cup) Nestlé Butterscotch Morsels
2 measuring tablespoons corn syrup
2 measuring tablespoons butter
2 measuring teaspoons water
1¼ measuring teaspoons grated orange rind
¼ measuring teaspoon salt
1 cup finely ground nuts

GARNISH

Whipped cream

CRÊPES: In a small bowl, combine milk, pancake mix, egg and oil; beat until mixture is smooth. Heat an 8-inch crêpe pan or skillet; brush with butter. For each crêpe, pour about 3 measuring tablespoons batter into pan; turn and tip pan immediately to coat bottom. Cook 10 to 15 seconds until lightly browned and set on top; turn and cook other side. Remove crêpe to a heated platter. Repeat with remaining batter. Spread 1 rounded measuring tablespoonful Butterscotch-Nut Filling (below) over each crêpe. Fold into triangles or roll up jelly-roll fashion; place on a serving platter. Spoon remaining filling over crêpes and serve with whipped cream.

BUTTERSCOTCH-NUT FILLING: Over hot (not boiling) water, combine Nestlé Butterscotch Morsels, corn syrup, butter, water, orange rind and salt; stir until morsels melt and mixture is smooth. Add nuts; mix well.

Makes 8 filled crêpes

CHOCOLATE-NUT CRÊPES: In the filling, substitute one 6-ounce package (1 cup) Nestlé Semi-Sweet Real Chocolate Morsels for Nestlé Butterscotch Morsels, and vanilla extract for grated orange rind.

Party Chocolate Crêpes

CRÊPES

1   6-ounce package (1 cup) Nestlé Semi-Sweet Real
    Chocolate Morsels
3   measuring tablespoons butter
1   cup *unsifted* flour
1   cup sifted confectioners' sugar
4   eggs
½   cup milk
½   cup water
1   measuring tablespoon vanilla extract
1   measuring teaspoon salt
    Melted butter
    Confectioners' sugar

ORANGE CREAM CHEESE FILLING

3   8-ounce packages cream cheese, softened
¾   cup sifted confectioners' sugar
½   cup milk
2   measuring tablespoons grated orange rind

CRÊPES: Over hot (not boiling) water, combine Nestlé Semi-Sweet Real Chocolate Morsels and butter; heat until morsels melt and mixture is smooth. Remove from heat; cool slightly. In blender container, combine cooled chocolate mixture, flour, confectioners' sugar, eggs, milk, water, vanilla extract and salt; blend at medium speed until smooth (about 2 minutes), scraping sides of container when necessary. Brush a 6- or 8-inch crêpe pan or skillet with melted butter. When butter begins to sizzle, pour about 3 measuring tablespoonfuls batter into pan; turn and tip pan immediately to coat bottom. Cook until top of crêpe begins to dry (about 20 seconds); turn and cook a few seconds. Remove from pan. Repeat with remaining batter. Spread 2 level measuring tablespoonfuls Orange Cream Cheese Filling (below) over each crêpe. Roll up jelly-roll fashion; place on a platter. Dust with confectioners' sugar.

ORANGE CREAM CHEESE FILLING: In a large bowl, combine cream cheese, confectioners' sugar, milk and grated orange rind; beat until smooth and creamy.

Makes 15 servings (30 filled crêpes)

Butterscotch-Nut Crêpes
Party Chocolate Crêpes

Chocolate-Butterscotch Roll

CAKE

1   6-ounce package (1 cup) Nestlé Semi-Sweet Real
     Chocolate Morsels
1/3 cup water
1   measuring teaspoon baking soda
4   eggs, separated
1/2 cup sugar
1   measuring teaspoon vanilla extract
1/4 measuring teaspoon salt
1/2 cup *unsifted* flour
     Confectioners' sugar

BUTTERSCOTCH FLUFF FILLING

1/2 cup orange juice
1   envelope (1 measuring tablespoon) unflavored gelatin
1/4 measuring teaspoon salt
3   eggs, separated
1   6-ounce package (1 cup) Nestlé Butterscotch Morsels
1/3 cup sugar

BUTTERSCOTCH SAUCE

1/4 cup orange juice
1/4 cup light corn syrup
1   measuring tablespoon cornstarch
1/8 measuring teaspoon salt
1/4 cup Nestlé Butterscotch Morsels (reserved from filling)
1   measuring tablespoon brandy

CAKE: Preheat oven to 375°F. Over hot (not boiling) water, combine Nestlé Semi-Sweet Real Chocolate Morsels and water; heat until morsels melt. Remove from heat. Stir in baking soda. In a small bowl, combine egg yolks, sugar, vanilla extract and salt. Beat at high speed until thick and lemon colored (about 5 minutes). Beat in melted chocolate mixture. Gradually add flour, 2 tablespoons at a time. In a small bowl, beat egg whites until stiff but not dry. Fold into chocolate mixture. Pour into greased and waxed paper lined 15x10x1-inch baking pan. Bake 15 minutes. Loosen edges and turn out immediately onto a towel sprinkled with confectioners' sugar. Remove paper. Trim edges. Starting with 10-inch edge, roll cake in towel. Cool on rack. Unroll carefully. Spread with Butterscotch Fluff Filling (right). Starting with 10-inch edge, roll up again; place seam side down on platter. Chill thoroughly. To serve, cut in 1-inch slices. Spoon on Butterscotch Sauce (right).

BUTTERSCOTCH FLUFF FILLING: In a medium saucepan, combine orange juice, gelatin, salt and egg yolks. Cook over medium heat until gelatin dissolves. Remove from heat. Add ¾ cup Nestlé Butterscotch Morsels; stir until morsels melt and mixture is smooth. In a small bowl, beat egg whites until soft peaks form. Gradually add sugar, beating until stiff peaks form. Fold into morsel mixture. Chill until set (about 1 hour).

BUTTERSCOTCH SAUCE: In a small saucepan, combine orange juice, corn syrup, corn starch and salt. Heat, stirring constantly, until mixture thickens. Add remaining ¼ cup Nestlé Butterscotch Morsels and stir until melted. Remove from heat; stir in brandy.

Makes one 10-inch cake roll

Note: Cake is very tender and may crack unless rolled very gently and loosely.

Brownie Torte

1   **12-ounce package (2 cups) Nestlé Semi-Sweet Real Chocolate Morsels**
1   **cup butter**
1½ **cups sugar**
4   **eggs**
1½ **cups *unsifted* flour**
1   **cup chopped nuts**
2   **cups heavy cream**
3   **measuring tablespoons confectioners' sugar**

Preheat oven to 375°F. Combine Nestlé Semi-Sweet Real Chocolate Morsels and butter over hot (not boiling) water; heat until morsels melt and mixture is smooth. Pour into a large bowl. Mix in sugar. Add eggs, one at a time, beating well after each addition. Gradually blend in flour. Stir in nuts. Pour into three greased and floured 9-inch round cake pans. Bake 15 to 20 minutes. Cool 10 minutes. Remove from pans; cool completely. In a large bowl, combine heavy cream and confectioners' sugar; beat until stiff peaks form. To assemble, spread a third of the whipped cream over each of 2 brownie layers. Decorate third layer with dollops of remaining whipped cream or pipe through pastry tube. Stack layers, placing decorated layer on top. Chill in refrigerator until ready to serve.

Makes one 9-inch torte

Heavenly Butterscotch Torte

CAKE

1	6-ounce package (1 cup) Nestlé Butterscotch Morsels
2	cups *unsifted* flour
1	measuring teaspoon baking soda
1	measuring teaspoon baking powder
1	measuring teaspoon mace
½	measuring teaspoon salt
1	cup sugar
¾	cup vegetable oil
1	measuring teaspoon vanilla extract
3	eggs
1	cup buttermilk or sour milk*
¼	cup orange liqueur or orange juice

CHOCOLATE ANGEL FROSTING

1	6-ounce package (1 cup) Nestlé Semi-Sweet Real Chocolate Morsels
½	cup sour cream
1	measuring teaspoon vanilla extract
¼	measuring teaspoon salt
2½	cups sifted confectioners' sugar

CAKE: Preheat oven to 350°F. Melt Nestlé Butterscotch Morsels over hot (not boiling) water. In a small bowl, combine flour, baking soda, baking powder, mace and salt; set aside. In a large bowl, combine sugar, oil, melted butterscotch and vanilla extract; beat until creamy. Add eggs, one at a time, beating well after each addition. Blend in flour mixture alternately with buttermilk. Pour batter evenly into two greased and floured 9-inch round cake pans. Bake 45 minutes. Cool 10 minutes. Remove from pans; cool completely. Using a long, thin serrated knife, slice each layer in half crosswise and sprinkle each with 1 measuring tablespoon orange liqueur or juice. Spread top of each layer (not sides) with Chocolate Angel Frosting (below).

CHOCOLATE ANGEL FROSTING: Melt Nestlé Semi-Sweet Real Chocolate Morsels over hot (not boiling) water. Transfer to a small bowl. Blend in sour cream, vanilla extract and salt. Gradually beat in confectioners' sugar; mix until creamy and smooth.

Makes one 9-inch torte

To make sour milk: Combine 1 measuring tablespoon vinegar or lemon juice and enough sweet milk to equal 1 cup. Let stand 5 minutes.

Chocolate-Meringue Nut Torte

MERINGUE-NUT LAYERS

3	egg whites
¼	measuring teaspoon salt
¾	cup firmly packed brown sugar
2	cups ground toasted almonds

CHOCOLATE FILLING

1	7½-ounce jar marshmallow cream
2	to 4 measuring tablespoons bourbon
1	6-ounce package (1 cup) Nestlé Semi-Sweet Real Chocolate Morsels
3	egg yolks
1	cup heavy cream, whipped

MERINGUE-NUT LAYERS: Cut four 8-inch circles of brown paper or parchment paper; place on large cookie sheet. Set aside. Preheat oven to 300°F. In a small bowl, combine egg whites and salt; beat until foamy. Gradually beat in brown sugar until stiff peaks form; fold in almonds. Spread ¾ cup meringue-nut mixture evenly on each paper circle, leaving a border of paper ¼ inch wide. Bake 20 to 25 minutes. Cool completely. Very carefully, so as not to break edges, remove paper from each layer. Place one layer on cake plate; spread ¾ cup Chocolate Filling (below) over top. Repeat with 2 more layers. Place fourth layer on top and garnish with dollops of remaining Chocolate Filling or pipe through pastry tube. Refrigerate until ready to serve.

CHOCOLATE FILLING: In a small bowl, combine marshmallow cream and bourbon; set aside. Melt Nestlé Semi-Sweet Real Chocolate Morsels over hot (not boiling) water; set aside. In a small bowl, beat egg yolks until thick (about 5 minutes); gradually add melted chocolate, stirring rapidly and constantly. Blend chocolate mixture into marshmallow mixture, stirring until smooth. Transfer to a large bowl. Chill in refrigerator 45 minutes (or over ice bath 15 to 20 minutes) until mixture is slightly thickened. Gently fold in whipped cream.

Makes one 9-inch torte

Quick Party Log, garnished with
Chocolate Curls and Meringue Mushrooms

Quick Party Log

1   12-ounce package (2 cups) Nestlé Semi-Sweet Real
     Chocolate Morsels
1   cup sour cream
1   measuring teaspoon vanilla extract
1/4 measuring teaspoon salt
3   cups sifted confectioners' sugar
2   11½-ounce frozen pound cakes, thawed
     Chocolate Curls and/or chocolate shavings (optional)
     Meringue Mushrooms (optional)

Melt Nestlé Semi-Sweet Real Chocolate Morsels over hot (not boiling) water. Transfer to a small bowl; cool 5 minutes. Blend in sour cream, vanilla extract and salt. Gradually add confectioners' sugar; beat until smooth. Set frosting aside.

Place pound cakes end to end to form one long cake. To form a log-shaped cake, round off edges by running a sharp knife down length of cake, slicing off all four corner edges (cake should resemble a cylinder). Cut cake crosswise into three layers. Fill and frost cake with prepared frosting. Run tines of fork lengthwise through frosting to simulate bark. Garnish with Chocolate Curls (below), chocolate shavings and Meringue Mushrooms (page 134), if desired.

Makes 16 slices

Chocolate Curls

1   12-ounce package (2 cups) Nestlé Semi-Sweet Real
     Chocolate Morsels
1/4 cup vegetable shortening

Over hot (not boiling) water, combine Nestlé Semi-Sweet Real Chocolate Morsels and vegetable shortening; stir until morsels melt and mixture is smooth. Pour into foil-lined 9x5x3-inch loaf pan. Chill until firm (about 2 hours). Remove foil from chocolate block. Make chocolate curls using one of the following: vegetable peeler, cheese slicer, cheese plane, lemon zester or butter curler.* Place on cookie sheet; chill until ready to use.

Makes 1¼ cups melted chocolate

*If chocolate appears too brittle to curl, let stand at room temperature 30 minutes before making Chocolate Curls.

Meringue Mushrooms

2   egg whites, at room temperature
⅛   measuring teaspoon salt
⅛   measuring teaspoon cream of tartar
¼   measuring teaspoon vanilla extract
½   cup sugar
     Nestlé Quik Chocolate Flavor
1   6-ounce package (1 cup) Nestlé Semi-Sweet Real
     Chocolate Morsels, melted (optional)

Preheat oven to 250°F. In a small bowl, beat egg whites until foamy. Add salt, cream of tartar and vanilla extract; beat until soft peaks form. Gradually add sugar, 2 tablespoons at a time, beating at high speed until stiff peaks form. Fill a pastry bag fitted with large writing tip with meringue. Pipe 15 mounds resembling mushroom caps (1 to 1½ inches in diameter) onto foil-lined cookie sheet. On another foil-lined cookie sheet, pipe 15 "mushroom stems" (1 to 1½ inches long). Lightly sift Quik evenly over caps and stems. Bake 25 to 35 minutes. Cool completely. To remove, peel back foil or loosen with metal spatula. Make a small hole in bottom of each cap. Insert pointed end of stem into hole. Bottoms of caps may be decorated with melted Nestlé Semi-Sweet Real Chocolate Morsels, if desired. Store in tightly covered container.

Makes 15 to 20 assorted-size meringue mushrooms

Old-Fashioned Mocha Shake

1   **cup milk**
2   **envelopes (2 ounces) Nestlé Choco-bake**
1   **measuring teaspoon vanilla extract**
1½ **cups coffee ice cream**

In blender container, combine milk, Choco-bake and vanilla extract; process at high speed until smooth, about 15 seconds. Add ice cream; blend until smooth. Serve immediately.

Makes 3 8-ounce servings

Note: Chocolate flecks will be dispersed throughout shake.

Rich Hot Chocolate

1   **6-ounce package (1 cup) Nestlé Semi-Sweet Real Chocolate Morsels**
1   **cup water**
2½ **cups milk**
1½ **cups heavy cream**
    Dash salt
2   **measuring tablespoons brandy or 1 measuring tablespoon instant coffee (optional)**

Over hot (not boiling) water, combine Nestlé Semi-Sweet Real Chocolate Morsels and water; heat until morsels melt and mixture is smooth. In a large saucepan, combine milk, cream and salt; bring *just to a boil.* Add chocolate mixture to milk mixture; stir until heated through. Stir in brandy or coffee, if desired, for added flavor.

Makes 6 servings

Hot Chocolate

1   **quart scalded milk, divided**
2   **envelopes (2 ounces) Nestlé Choco-bake, divided**
6   **measuring tablespoons sugar, divided**

In blender container, combine half the milk, 1 envelope Nestlé Choco-bake and half the sugar; process at high speed about 15 seconds. Pour into serving cups. Repeat with remaining ingredients. Serve immediately.

Makes 6 to 8 servings

Easy Chocolate Fondue

1   6-ounce package (1 cup) Nestlé Semi-Sweet Real
     Chocolate Morsels
½   cup corn syrup
1   measuring teaspoon vanilla extract
     Dash salt
2   to 3 measuring tablespoons brandy
     Bite-size pieces fruit (apples, bananas, seedless grapes,
       fresh strawberries, maraschino cherries or mandarin
       orange segments)
     Pound cake, cut into cubes
     Ground nuts or toasted shredded coconut (optional)

Combine Nestlé Semi-Sweet Real Chocolate Morsels, corn syrup, vanilla extract and salt in an electric fondue pot or a large saucepan. Stir over medium heat until morsels melt and mixture is smooth. Add brandy; mix well. Serve with your favorite fruit dippers and/or pound cake cubes. After dipping in chocolate, coat with ground nuts or shredded coconut, if desired.

Makes 1 cup fondue

Indian Pudding

6   measuring tablespoons yellow cornmeal
¾   measuring teaspoon cinnamon
½   measuring teaspoon ginger
¼   measuring teaspoon nutmeg
2½ cups milk
1   6-ounce package (1 cup) Nestlé Butterscotch Morsels
3   eggs
¼   cup molasses
     Sweetened whipped cream

Preheat oven to 350°F. In a small bowl, combine cornmeal, cinnamon, ginger and nutmeg; set aside. In a large saucepan, heat milk until it begins to foam around the edges. Gradually add cornmeal mixture. Cook, stirring constantly with a wire whisk, until mixture boils and becomes thickened; remove from heat. Add Nestlé Butterscotch Morsels; stir until morsels melt and mixture is smooth. Cool 10 minutes at room temperature. In a small bowl, combine eggs and molasses; beat until thick (about 2 to 3 minutes). Gradually stir into butterscotch mixture. Pour into 1½-quart casserole. Bake 45 to 50 minutes. Serve immediately with whipped cream.

Makes 6 to 8 servings

Easy Chocolate Fondue

Butterscotch-Apple Crisp

FILLING

 1 **measuring tablespoon lemon juice**
 8 **cups pared, cored and sliced tart cooking apples or 3
    20-ounce cans sliced apples**
 1 **cup sugar**
 ½ **cup *unsifted* flour**
 2 **measuring teaspoons cinnamon**
 ⅛ **measuring teaspoon salt**

TOPPING

 1 **12-ounce package (2 cups) Nestlé Butterscotch Morsels**
 ½ **cup butter**
1½ **cups *unsifted* flour**
 ¼ **measuring teaspoon salt**
 ¼ **measuring teaspoon mace**
    **Heavy cream, sweetened whipped cream or vanilla ice
    cream (optional)**

FILLING: Preheat oven to 375°F. In a large bowl, combine lemon juice and sliced apples; toss until well coated. Stir in sugar, flour, cinnamon and salt; mix well. Turn into greased 13x9x2-inch baking pan; spread evenly. Bake 20 minutes. Crumble topping (below) over top of hot apples. Return to oven; bake 25 minutes. Serve warm with heavy cream, sweetened whipped cream or vanilla ice cream, if desired.

TOPPING: Over hot (not boiling) water, combine Nestlé Butterscotch Morsels and butter; stir until morsels melt and mixture is smooth. Remove from heat. With a fork, stir in flour, salt and mace until flour is just blended and mixture forms a large crumb.

Makes 12 servings

Rescue breakfasts from boredom and offer a sweet surprise: warm Butterscotch-Apple Crisp (make ahead; reheat in the morning) served with a splash of heavy cream. Who'll miss the toast?

Butterscotch Bread Pudding

5   slices white bread, cut into 1-inch cubes
1   apple, pared and sliced
½   cup chopped nuts
3   cups milk
1   6-ounce package (1 cup) Nestlé Butterscotch Morsels
3   eggs
¼   cup firmly packed brown sugar
1   measuring teaspoon vanilla extract
½   measuring teaspoon cinnamon
¼   measuring teaspoon mace
¼   measuring teaspoon salt
    Heavy cream (optional)

Preheat oven to 350°F. Place bread cubes and apple slices on bottom of 8-inch square baking pan; sprinkle with nuts. In a large saucepan, combine milk and Nestlé Butterscotch Morsels; place over medium heat until morsels melt and mixture is smooth. In a small bowl, combine eggs, brown sugar, vanilla extract, cinnamon, mace and salt; beat well. Stir into butterscotch-milk mixture. Pour over bread cubes and apple slices. Set square pan into a large roasting pan; pour boiling water in roasting pan to depth of 1 inch. Bake 45 minutes or until knife inserted in center comes out clean. Cool 10 minutes. Serve with heavy cream, if desired.

Makes 6 servings

From top: Holiday Steamed Pudding,
Miniature Chocolate Fruitcakes,
Sherry Fruitcake

Holiday Steamed Pudding

PUDDING

1   **6-ounce package (1 cup) Nestlé Semi-Sweet Real Chocolate Morsels**
1½   cups chopped pecans
1   cup currants
1   cup uncooked quick oats
¾   cup chopped candied cherries
¾   cup *unsifted* flour
¾   cup sugar
2   measuring teaspoons cinnamon
1¼   measuring teaspoons baking soda
¾   measuring teaspoon salt
1   cup buttermilk or sour milk (see note, page 130)
2   measuring teaspoons vanilla extract

BRANDIED HARD SAUCE

1   5¼-ounce jar hard sauce
2   eggs
1   measuring tablespoon milk
1   measuring tablespoon brandy

PUDDING: Melt Nestlé Semi-Sweet Real Chocolate Morsels over hot (not boiling) water; remove from heat and set aside. In a large bowl, combine pecans, currants, oats, candied cherries, flour, sugar, cinnamon, baking soda and salt; toss together. Add melted chocolate, buttermilk and vanilla extract; mix well. Press into greased 5- to 6-cup heatproof mold. Cover tightly with foil. Place covered mold on rack or trivet in a deep kettle or roasting pan. Pour boiling water into kettle halfway up side of mold (water should not touch foil cover). Cover kettle; simmer over low heat 2 hours or until toothpick inserted in center comes out clean. Cool 10 minutes; remove from mold and cool completely. If using as a gift, return pudding to cleaned mold.

To reheat, cover mold with foil and bake at 350°F. for 30 to 45 minutes. Serve warm with Brandied Hard Sauce (below), or sweetened whipped cream or ice cream.

BRANDIED HARD SAUCE: In a small bowl, combine hard sauce, eggs, milk and brandy; beat until creamy. Refrigerate.

Makes 8 servings pudding and about 1⅓ cups sauce

Sauces, Frostings and Glazes

Sauces for ice creams and puddings, frostings for cakes... and the little ones underfoot trying to lick the bowl. What pleasant memories to have, what pleasant times to pass... talking and working in the quiet intimacy of your kitchen, sharing its warmth and gaiety with your children.

In time the little ones will be as interested in learning how to make your "just plain good" sauces and frostings as they are in helping to clean out the bowl. That is the stuff of traditions. As your mother passed these pleasures and skills to you, so will you to your own children and they to theirs.

Center: Rich Hot Chocolate, Blender Chocolate Ice Cream. Ice cream sauces, top to bottom: Hot Creamy Fudge Sauce, Hot Chocolate Sauce, Orange-Butterscotch Sauce with Chocolate Dessert Waffle.

Hot Chocolate Sauce

¾ **cup sugar**
¼ **cup butter**
2 **envelopes (2 ounces) Nestlé Choco-bake**
2 **measuring tablespoons light corn syrup**
   Dash of salt
¼ **cup milk**
2 **measuring teaspoons vanilla extract**

In a small saucepan, combine sugar, butter, Nestlé Choco-bake, corn syrup and salt; mix well. Cook over medium heat, stirring constantly, until sugar dissolves. Add milk; bring to a boil, stirring constantly. Remove from heat; stir in vanilla extract. Serve warm over ice cream or cake.

Makes 1 cup sauce

Orange-Butterscotch Sauce

1 **6-ounce package (1 cup) Nestlé Butterscotch Morsels**
¼ **cup evaporated milk**
¼ **measuring teaspoon orange extract**

Melt Nestlé Butterscotch Morsels over hot (not boiling) water. Stir in evaporated milk and orange extract. Blend mixture with a fork or wire whisk until smooth. Serve warm over ice cream or cake.

Makes ¾ cup sauce

Hot Creamy Fudge Sauce

½ **cup milk**
¼ **cup butter**
¼ **measuring teaspoon salt**
1 **11½-ounce package (2 cups) Nestlé Milk Chocolate Morsels**
1 **measuring teaspoon vanilla extract**

Over hot (not boiling) water, combine milk, butter and salt; heat until butter melts. Add Nestlé Milk Chocolate Morsels; stir until morsels melt and mixture is smooth. Remove from heat; stir in vanilla extract. Serve warm over ice cream, cake, waffles or pancakes.

Makes 1½ cups sauce

Chocolate Skillet Sauce

¼ **cup butter**
1 **cup coarsely chopped nuts**
1 **6-ounce package (1 cup) Nestlé Semi-Sweet Real**
   Chocolate Morsels

Melt butter in a large skillet.* Add nuts and cook until browned,
stirring constantly to prevent scorching. Remove from heat. Add
Nestlé Semi-Sweet Real Chocolate Morsels and stir until morsels
melt and mixture is blended. Serve warm over ice cream.

Makes 1¼ cups sauce

* This recipe may be made in an electric skillet set at 350°F.

*BUTTERSCOTCH SKILLET SAUCE: Substitute one 6-ounce
package (1 cup) Nestlé Butterscotch Morsels for chocolate morsels.*

*MILK CHOCOLATE SKILLET SAUCE: Increase butter to ½ cup
and nuts to 2 cups. Substitute one 11½-ounce package (2 cups)
Nestlé Milk Chocolate Morsels for semi-sweet chocolate morsels.*

Makes 2½ cups sauce

Hot Mocha Ice Cream Sauce

1 **6-ounce package (1 cup) Nestlé Semi-Sweet Real**
   Chocolate Morsels
¾ **cup corn syrup**
¼ **cup milk**
2 **measuring tablespoons butter**
1 **measuring teaspoon instant coffee**

In a small saucepan, combine Nestlé Semi-Sweet Real Chocolate
Morsels and corn syrup; heat over low heat until morsels melt and
mixture is smooth. Add milk, butter and coffee; stir until well
blended. Remove from heat; cool 5 minutes. Serve warm over ice
cream or cake.

Makes 1½ cups sauce

Cooked Chocolate Frosting

1 **cup sugar**
4 **envelopes (4 ounces) Nestlé Choco-bake**
⅔ **cup heavy cream**
¼ **cup water**
2 **measuring tablespoons corn syrup**
1 **egg, slightly beaten**
1 **measuring teaspoon vanilla extract**

In a large saucepan, combine sugar, Nestlé Choco-bake, cream, water and corn syrup. Cook over moderate heat, stirring constantly, until sugar dissolves. Cook without stirring 6 minutes. Remove from heat. Blend about 3 measuring tablespoons chocolate mixture into egg and return to chocolate mixture. Stir in vanilla extract. Cook, stirring constantly, over moderate heat, about 1 minute or until thick. Cool completely before frosting cake. Fills and frosts two 8-inch layers or one 13x9x2-inch cake.

Makes about 2 cups frosting

Sour Cream Velvet Frosting

1 **12-ounce package (2 cups) Nestlé Semi-Sweet Real Chocolate Morsels**
⅔ **cup sour cream**
1 **measuring teaspoon vanilla extract**
¼ **measuring teaspoon salt**
3 **cups sifted confectioners' sugar**

Melt Nestlé Semi-Sweet Real Chocolate Morsels over hot (not boiling) water; transfer to a large bowl and cool 5 minutes. Blend in sour cream, vanilla extract and salt. Gradually beat in confectioners' sugar; beat until smooth and creamy. Fills and frosts two 8- or 9-inch cake layers.

Makes 2⅔ cups frosting

Creamy Butterscotch Frosting

1   6-ounce package (1 cup) Nestlé Butterscotch Morsels
1   measuring tablespoon water
1   8-ounce package cream cheese, softened
⅛   measuring teaspoon salt
3   cups sifted confectioners' sugar

Over hot (not boiling) water, combine Nestlé Butterscotch Morsels and water; stir until morsels melt and mixture is smooth. Remove from heat. In a small bowl, combine cream cheese and salt; beat until creamy. Blend in melted butterscotch. Gradually add confectioners' sugar. Beat until smooth. Fills and frosts two 8- or 9-inch cake layers.

Makes 2½ cups frosting

Chocolate Butter Frosting

¼   cup milk
2   measuring tablespoons butter
⅛   measuring teaspoon salt
1   6-ounce package (1 cup) Nestlé Semi-Sweet Real
      Chocolate Morsels
1   measuring teaspoon vanilla extract
1½ cups sifted confectioners' sugar
1   to 2 measuring teaspoons milk

In a medium saucepan, combine ¼ cup milk, butter and salt; bring to a boil over medium heat. Remove from heat. Add Nestlé Semi-Sweet Real Chocolate Morsels and vanilla extract; stir until morsels melt and mixture is smooth. Blend in confectioners' sugar. Stir in 1 to 2 measuring teaspoons milk until mixture is of spreading consistency. Beat well. Frosts one 13x9x2-inch cake.

Makes 1⅓ cups frosting

Note: Frosting appears thin but does cling nicely to cake.

Butterscotch-Grapefruit Cupcakes and a medley of cupcakes topped with Easy Chocolate Glaze and Creamy Butterscotch Frosting

149

Rich Chocolate Cream Frosting

1   12-ounce package (2 cups) Nestlé Semi-Sweet Real
    Chocolate Morsels
1   8-ounce package cream cheese, softened
1   measuring teaspoon vanilla extract
½   measuring teaspoon salt
3¼ cups sifted confectioners' sugar
2   measuring tablespoons milk

Melt Nestlé Semi-Sweet Real Chocolate Morsels over hot (not boiling) water; remove from heat. In a large bowl, combine melted chocolate, cream cheese, vanilla extract and salt; beat well. Beat in confectioners' sugar alternately with milk. Fills and frosts two 8- or 9-inch cake layers.

Makes 3 cups frosting

Creamy Mocha Frosting

1   11½-ounce package (2 cups) Nestlé Milk Chocolate
    Morsels
1   measuring teaspoon instant coffee
⅔   cup sour cream
1   measuring teaspoon vanilla extract
¼   measuring teaspoon salt
3   cups sifted confectioners' sugar

Melt Nestlé Milk Chocolate Morsels over hot (not boiling) water; remove from heat. Stir in coffee; cool 10 minutes. In a small bowl, combine melted chocolate mixture, sour cream, vanilla extract and salt; beat well. Gradually beat in confectioners' sugar. Fills and frosts two 8- or 9-inch cake layers.

Makes 3 cups frosting

A hurry-up hint: Frost any cupcake fast by dipping the top lightly into a fluffy (not runny) frosting such as Sour Cream Velvet Frosting (page 147), Creamy Butterscotch Frosting (page 148) or Creamy Mocha Frosting (page 150). Nimble trick for little fingers, too!

Easy Chocolate Glaze

½   cup evaporated milk
     Dash salt
1   6-ounce package (1 cup) Nestlé Semi-Sweet Real
     Chocolate Morsels
1   measuring teaspoon vanilla extract

In a small saucepan, combine evaporated milk and salt; bring *just to
a boil* over medium heat, stirring constantly. Add Nestlé Semi-
Sweet Real Chocolate Morsels and vanilla extract; stir until morsels
melt and mixture is smooth. Cool at room temperature until thick
enough to spread (about 30 minutes).

Makes 1 cup glaze

Butterscotch Orange Glaze

1   6-ounce package (1 cup) Nestlé Butterscotch Morsels
1   measuring teaspoon vegetable oil
1   measuring teaspoon grated orange rind
2   measuring tablespoons orange juice

Over hot (not boiling) water, combine Nestlé Butterscotch Morsels
and vegetable oil; stir until morsels melt. Remove from heat. Stir in
orange rind and juice. Use as a glaze for cakes, cupcakes or cookies.

Makes ⅔ cup glaze

152

Three Chocolate Surprises

Chocolátl, *or bitter drink, is what the Aztecs called it, and their emperor Montezuma is said to have consumed fifty cups of it a day. It was the Spanish who added cinnamon and sugar and drank it hot. Their descendants, who settled Mexico and intermarried with the Indians, added chocolate to sauces for meat and poultry.*

And thus, in a line of direct descent, we share the taste of both cultures and the knowledge that chocolate is not for desserts alone, but plays a varied—and always delicious—role in the traditions of good cooking.

Chili

2 measuring tablespoons vegetable oil
1 medium onion, chopped
2 garlic cloves, minced
1 pound ground beef
1 16-ounce can kidney beans, drained
1 16-ounce can tomato puree
1 6-ounce can tomato paste
1 4-ounce can chopped green chili peppers, seeded and
    drained
½ cup water
2 envelopes (2 ounces) Nestlé Choco-bake, divided
2 measuring tablespoons chili powder
1 measuring tablespoon beef-flavored instant bouillon

Heat oil in a large skillet; add onion and garlic and sauté until tender. Add ground beef; cook over medium heat until meat is evenly browned. Drain off excess fat. Stir in beans, tomato puree, tomato paste, chili peppers, water, 1 envelope Nestlé Choco-bake, chili powder and bouillon; mix well. Simmer uncovered 30 minutes, stirring occasionally. Stir in remaining Nestlé Choco-bake and heat through. Serve with corn chips or over hot rice.

Makes 4 to 6 servings

The mystery ingredient: Why would chocolate—of all things—wind up in a dish such as Chili? To us, chocolate is inseparably associated with sweets and desserts, but its use in main dishes is traditional in Mexican cooking. Enhancing the spices, enlivening other ingredients, chocolate becomes an instrument in an exciting and harmonious orchestration of tastes.

Chili, Chicken Mole

Chicken Mole

CHICKEN

⅓   cup *unsifted* flour
3   measuring tablespoons chili powder, divided
2   measuring teaspoons salt
½   measuring teaspoon pepper
2   broiler-fryers (2½ to 3 pounds each), cut up
3   measuring tablespoons vegetable oil
1   cup chopped onion
3   garlic cloves, minced
¼   cup water

CHOCOLATE MOLE SAUCE

1   10-ounce can tomatoes and green chilies
1   cup tomato puree
1   6-ounce package (1 cup) Nestlé Semi-Sweet Real
     Chocolate Morsels
1   measuring teaspoon chicken-flavored instant bouillon (or
     1 cube, crushed)

GARNISH

1   cup chopped peanuts

CHICKEN: In a large bowl or plastic bag, combine flour, 1 measuring tablespoon chili powder, the salt and pepper. Add chicken pieces (2 to 3 at a time); coat well. Heat oil in a large skillet; brown half the chicken pieces on all sides over medium heat. Drain thoroughly on paper towels. Repeat with remaining chicken. In same skillet, sauté onion and garlic until golden. Return chicken to skillet. Add the water; simmer, covered, over medium heat about 35 to 40 minutes or until chicken is tender. Transfer to a serving platter and top with Chocolate Mole Sauce (below). Garnish each serving with chopped peanuts.

CHOCOLATE MOLE SAUCE: In a small saucepan, combine tomatoes and green chilies, tomato puree, Nestlé Semi-Sweet Real Chocolate Morsels, remaining chili powder and bouillon. Cook over low heat until morsels melt and sauce is heated through.

Makes 6 to 8 servings and 3⅓ cups sauce

Note: This mole is milder in flavor than a traditional Mexican mole.

Chocolate Fruit Soup

1   6-ounce package (1 cup) Nestlé Semi-Sweet Real
    Chocolate Morsels, divided
1   cup milk
1   10-ounce package frozen raspberries, drained, or
    1 medium banana
1¼ cups heavy cream
½   measuring teaspoon vanilla extract
½   measuring teaspoon cinnamon
    Whipped cream (optional)

Place ½ cup Nestlé Semi-Sweet Real Chocolate Morsels in blender container; process at high speed about 15 seconds or until reduced to fine particles. Remove from blender and set aside. Over hot (not boiling) water, combine remaining Nestlé Semi-Sweet Real Chocolate Morsels and the milk; heat until morsels melt and mixture is combined. (Morsel-milk mixture will contain flecks of chocolate.) In blender container, combine morsel-milk mixture, raspberries or banana, cream, vanilla extract and cinnamon. Process at high speed until smooth (about 30 seconds). Pour soup through a fine sieve to remove raspberry seeds. Chill until ready to serve (at least 3 hours). Garnish with whipped cream and grated morsels.

Makes 4 servings

Index

Lotta
Jansdotter

Simple Sewing for Baby

Lotta
Jansdotter

Simple Sewing for Baby

24 Easy Projects for Newborns to Toddlers

Projects and Illustrations by Lotta Jansdotter
Photographs by Meiko Takechi Arquillos

CHRONICLE BOOKS
SAN FRANCISCO

Manufactured in China.

Designed by Tuesday
Technical writing and sewing by Laura Sewrey
Styling by Lotta Anderson

Library of Congress Cataloging-in-Publication Data:

Jansdotter, Lotta.
   Simple sewing for baby : 24 easy projects for newborns to toddlers / by Lotta Jansdotter ; photographs by Meiko
   Takechi Arquillos.
      p. cm.
      Includes index.
      ISBN: 978-0-8118-6548-7
      1. Sewing. 2. Infants' clothing. 3. Infants' supplies. I. Title.

   TT705.J33 2009
   646.4'06—dc22

                              2008026507

10 9 8 7 6 5 4 3 2

Chronicle Books LLC
680 Second Street
San Francisco, California 94107
www.chroniclebooks.com

Acknowledgments

I have worked with the cutest and most delightful little models for this book.
All the sweet babies and their parents have been SO very nice and lovely.
THANK YOU for all your help and for making this book happen:

eli gray culler, jason culler, allisyn levy,
zachary odunsi, ethan odunsi, sasadi odunsi, ade odunsi,
isabel marks, ezra marks, rachel schneider, ben marks,
eve olivia bowker, amanda z bowker, david bowker,
simon sherber brannan, moira brannan, jeremy sherber,
ella atkinson, maria boren,
matea salame', annika salame', philippe salame',
zoe taylor, josh taylor, lisa taylor,
august anderson, and nick anderson.

I am utterly grateful and happy for all the excellent and hard work from my team at
Chronicle Books and Tuesday. Mrs. Osanai: You are a delight. Thank you for your wonderful help.
Laura: I cannot thank you enough!!! and Meiko: You are simply a star: I love working with you!!!

Dedication
For August, the brave and sunny one.

Contents

Fashion
Bloomers 23

Fashion
Bib Kerchief 28

Fashion
Simple Dress 32

Fashion
Soft Hat and Scarf 54

Play
Soft Rattle 63

Play
Buddy 67

Home
Snuggler 87

Home
Bib 93

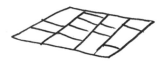

Home
Play Quilt with
Pocket 97

Home
Washcloths 111

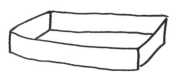

Home
Crib Bumper 112

Going Out
Diaper Bag 123

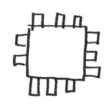

Introduction

When I became pregnant with baby August I was incredibly happy, of course. I was happy to be able to experience pregnancy, happy to experience motherhood, and also incredibly giddy about all the baby goods that I was now "allowed" to acquire.

A few months into the pregnancy, and after visits to various baby-gear shops, I realized that there isn't all that much cool or original stuff for somebody who doesn't like pink or light blue and doesn't want bows or duckies plastered on everything. Okay, there are some things, like sweet mittens, darling dresses, and diaper bags that are pretty great, but they will set you back an arm and a leg, and I just can't let myself spend that kind of money on something that will be used for only a few months. So I figured I would make some baby things myself. Not only will it save me money, I realized, but it's also more satisfying to make my own unique goods.

Because I didn't have a clue how to make my own baby items, I browsed shops and the Internet with hopes of finding some helpful and inspiring books. I didn't know what a little baby needs and why; if snaps are better than zippers; what sizes are suitable for which age; etcetera. Eventually I found some helpful Web sites and, thanks to my friends who already had some ankle biters, I made a list of necessities. It seemed like such a long list! Could it really be accurate?

I sewed a couple bibs and a blanket, and we received some very nice gifts for our future prince. After a few more months it was time for the arrival of our new family member.

Now it has been over a year since the boy arrived, and I'm having an action-packed, exhausting, and absolutely wonderful time. I am now also a year more experienced in the world of baby gear. It is amazing (and a tad unappealing) how caught up one can get in all the stroller debates, diaper pail options, and proper shoe choices.

I now know that there are many things you can cross off your shopping list. A baby has only a few basic requirements and doesn't need a bunch of crazy doodads. It is far too easy to get drawn into the world of nursery gadgets, and I try my best to resist.

Having said that: Some paraphernalia really is useful, and you certainly do need some supplies for your baby. Plus there are some items that make the whole experience a wee bit more fun and adorable. But I still cannot find very many creative and exciting how-to books for making your own baby goods, which is surprising considering that the baby accessories market is expanding rapidly.

So it was only natural for me to start planning a new sewing book with baby items in mind. Now I was armed with more insight and plenty of ideas about items that might be useful (and fun!) for babyhood.

My first American how-to book, **Simple Sewing** (Chronicle Books, 2007), was directed mainly toward beginners, but it was also for busy people who wanted some easy and stimulating ideas to get them motivated to sew. With **Simple Sewing for Baby**, I have a similar goal: Keep it simple. I have included suggestions for projects that are easy to make, many of which can be created in an evening or on a Saturday afternoon. I have also compiled projects that I found to be the most practical. (For example, all moms and dads absolutely need changing pads if they plan to leave the house with their babies in the next two years.) And some projects have been included just because they are cute and fun, such as the Book Mates (page 101) and Soft Rattle (page 63).

I encourage you all—nesting moms and dads, grandmothers-to-be, uncles—to customize these projects with your choice of fabrics. There are so many fabulous textiles on the market, and they're easily obtained from online stores. Embrace patterns, bold colors, and crazy motifs. Get creative with stencils and potato prints. Revolt against all the pinks and light blues of the baby world!

Before You Get Started

About Fabrics:

When sewing items for babies, it is best to use natural fibers such as cotton, linen, and wool. Natural fabrics allow the skin to breathe.

Cotton fabric has a high degree of strength, durability, and absorbency. A baby's clothing has to be washed over and over again, so cotton is a good choice. Items made out of cotton will last for a long time.

I also like using linen. Many people are intimidated by linen, thinking it is hard to take care of, but it actually isn't at all. Linen is an incredibly strong fiber that can be machine-washed. It gets softer after each use, which makes it very nice on a baby's skin. It does wrinkle easily, but that doesn't bother me at all; rumples add to linen's appeal, in my opinion.

Wool is a little bit trickier: It can be itchy if used for clothing, and it cannot be washed as easily as other natural fibers because it shrinks. In some of the projects for this book, I have opted to use cotton fleece instead of wool because fleece is soft and easy to work with. If you have a hard time finding cotton fleece, synthetic microfleece is easily available at fabric stores. Microfleece is indeed a man-made fiber, but it works well for certain baby items such as scarves and hats.

Fabric made out of bamboo is new, exciting material. It is known for its velvety softness and environmental friendliness. Hemp is another natural fiber that increasingly interests me. It comes in a variety of textures and thicknesses and is very durable.

Fabric Tips:

· Be sure to preshrink all your fabrics before cutting them. Many fabrics shrink when they are washed—and they do so at different rates! To spare yourself the great disappointment of having a finished piece ruined in the laundry, prior to getting started you should wash, dry, and press all your fabrics as you will the finished item.

· Be aware of the colorfastness of your fabrics. You don't want colors to bleed into each other. (This is another good reason to wash your fabrics prior to sewing them together.) The notions, ribbons, and trims also should be colorfast and washed.

· When cutting fabric, check the grain (the direction of the lengthwise and crosswise threads in a woven fabric). With knits, the grain can be seen in the lengthwise ribs. Often a pattern calls for matching the grain lines, so make sure the grain line marked on the pattern runs along the grain of your fabric.

When making items for babies and small children, it is very important to think of their safety.

Safety Tips:

· Make sure that you always secure seams properly so they won't unravel. For example, if you are making Book Mates (page 101), you do not want the stuffing to leak and get in the hands or mouth of a baby.

· If you use buttons or other trim, make super-sure that they are secured VERY well to prevent the baby or toddler from ripping (or gnawing) them off and choking on them.

· Use nontoxic inks when you are stenciling on projects.

· Tying a scarf or kerchief around a small baby's neck might seem scary, and rightfully so. I would not recommend for a newborn to wear such a thing. When the older babies and toddlers wear them make sure that they are supervised at all times, and never let them sleep wearing such articles.

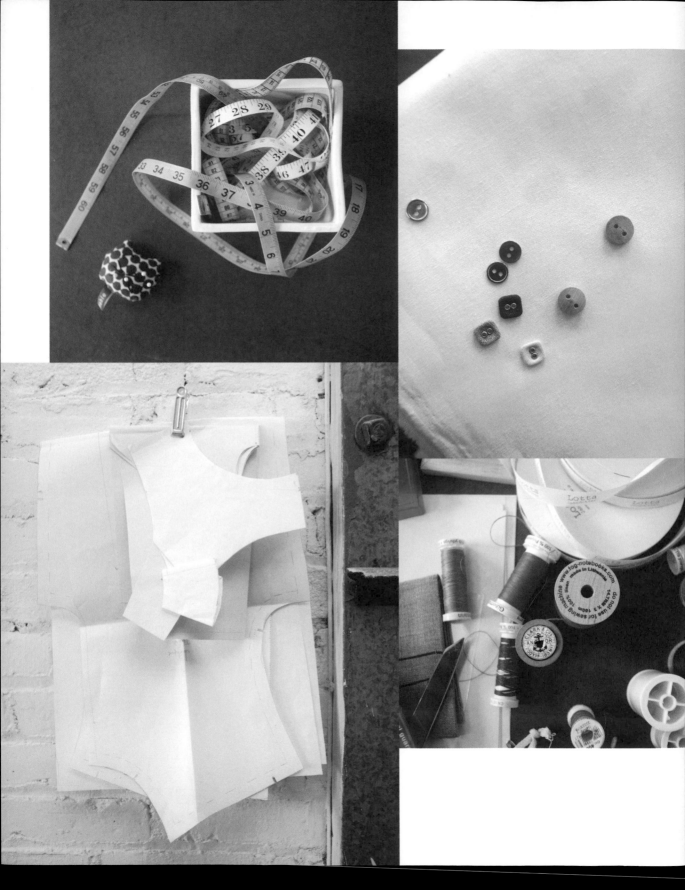

Sewing Equipment

Here is a list of tools needed to make the projects in this book:

Sewing machine with spare needles
Assorted threads for machine
Scissors (never cut paper with them—it makes them dull)
Seam ripper
Tape measure
Clear plastic ruler
Yardstick
Fabric marker
Fadeout marker or tailor's chalk
Straight pins and safety pins
Hand-sewing needles
Iron and ironing board
Spray bottle to hold water for steam pressing
Unsharpened pencil with an eraser on one end
Masking tape
Point turner (a large knitting needle or chopstick will also work well)

Not necessary, but can make your life easier:

Rotary cutter and mat
Pinking shears
Pincushion
Thimble

Bloomers

These things are so darling for any tush, whether a boy's or a girl's. Make some out of flannel for cold winter days, or thin cotton for outdoor play in the summer. You will find a pattern for this in two sizes: one for a baby, about one- to six-months-old, and one for a toddler, about six- to twelve-months-old. Cute, cute, cute!

Finished size:
Newborn to six months
Six to twelve months

Fabric:
¾ yard (44 in wide) /70 cm (114 cm wide) cotton

Supplies:
Pattern from the front pocket of this book
Scissors
Straight pins
Ruler
Fabric marker
Thread
Iron
Small safety pin
1 yard (¼ in wide) /90 cm (6 mm wide) elastic

Notes:
All seams are ½ in/12 mm unless otherwise noted. The seam allowance is included in the cutting instructions and pattern. Preshrink your fabric by washing, drying, and pressing it before you start.

Step 1: Cut out the pieces from the fabric

A: Cut out the pattern pieces provided at the front of this book.

B: Lay your fabric Right side up. Fold each selvedge edge to the center of the fabric; the selvedges will meet in the middle. Place the pattern pieces on the folds as marked and pin the pattern pieces to the fabric. Cut out the Bloomer pieces by following the solid cutting lines on the pattern.

C: You will need two bias strips for the leg binding. Unfold your fabric and on the Wrong side, at a 45-degree angle to the fabric's grain line, cut two strips that are 1½ in/3.8 cm wide x 14 in/36 cm long. Use your fabric marker to outline your strips. Cut them out along your markings. [figure 1]

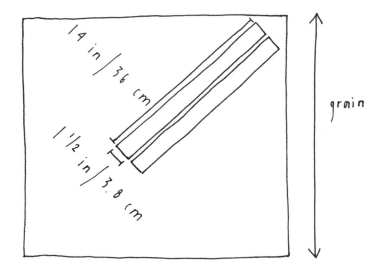

Figure 1

Step 2: Sew the bloomers together

A: Unfold all your pieces of fabric. With the Right sides together, place the front piece on top of the back piece. Align the side seams and pin them. Then align the crotch seams, and pin them. Sew each side seam, backstitching at the beginning and end. Sew across the crotch, backstitching at the beginning and end.

B: Trim the seam allowances to ¼ in/6 mm. Zigzag along the edge of the seam allowance to prevent fraying, being careful to not catch the straight seam in the zigzag. (If you are not able to zigzag, use pinking shears to trim the seams to ¼ in/6 mm. This will help slow the fraying of the seams.) Press each seam.

C: With the Wrong side of fabric facing you, fold the waist over ½ in/12 mm and press. Then fold over ½ in/12 mm again and press. Leaving a 2 in/5 cm opening over one of the side seams, pin along the folded edge. Machine-stitch close to the folded-under edge, making sure to leave open the 2 in/5 cm over the side seam, backstitching at the beginning and end of the seam.

D: Fold over and press ½ in/12 mm along one long side of each of the bias strips. Then, fold under ½ in/12 mm at one short end of the bias tape and press. With the Right sides together, and starting with the pressed-under end of the bias tape, pin the unfolded long side of the bias strip around each of the leg openings, starting at the crotch seam. Overlap the binding ¾ in/1.9 cm at the end and trim off any excess binding. Machine-stitch around each leg hole. Trim the seam allowance to ¼ in/6 mm and clip it, being careful not to clip through your seam.

E: Fold under and press the binding inside the leg holes. Pin the binding's folded edge to the inside of the bloomers, easing any wrinkles. Leave a 1½ in/3.8 cm opening at the crotch seam. You may need to smooth the binding with your fingers as you go to make it lie smoothly. Tuck the binding's raw end inside the folded end where the two ends meet so there are no raw edges. Machine-stitch closely to the folded edge of the binding, being sure to leave a 1½ in/3.8 cm opening at the crotch seam and backstitching at the beginning and end of the seam.

F: Attach a small safety pin to one end of the elastic. Insert the safety pin into the 2 in/5 cm opening at the waist. Thread the elastic through the waistband by pushing the safety pin along and easing the fabric over the pin. The fabric will gather up over the pin, but just keep pushing it over the pin and inching forward, allowing the elastic to be pulled inside the waistband. Make sure to keep the other end of the elastic from being pulled inside the waistband. Once the pin emerges back out of the opening, pin the ends of the elastic together. Pull the elastic to the waist size of the child. Lay one end of elastic over the other and pin. Machine-stitch the elastic together and trim the excess.

G: Slip the elastic inside the waistband and pin the opening closed. Machine-stitch the opening closed, being careful to not stitch over the elastic, backstitching at the beginning and end.

H: Repeat steps F and G for the leg openings.

Bib Kerchief

Here is a perfect item for the drooly baby in your life: a bib that looks like a bandana. It works like a bib, but it is much cuter than that. This couldn't possibly be easier to sew, so it will take you no time to churn out a batch of them—and they make great gifts! Soft cotton is a good fabric choice for this little item.

My son August went through three or four of these a day when he was drooling the most (at about five to eight months). Now he's teething, and he still drools—so I sewed several of these in different patterns to mix and match with his outfits.

These kerchiefs make cute little head scarves for your sweet peas, too. Why not make seven of them—one for each day of the week?

Finished size:
27 in/69 cm long x 9 in/23 cm wide

Fabric:
⅓ yard (44 in wide) /30 cm (114 cm wide) soft cotton fabric

Notes:
The seam allowance is included in the cutting instructions and pattern. Preshrink your fabric by washing, drying, and pressing it before you start.

Supplies:
Pattern from the front pocket of this book
Scissors
Straight pins
Iron
Thread

Step 1: Cut out the piece from the fabric

A: Cut out the pattern piece provided at the front of this book.

B: Pin the pattern to the fabric. Cut out the pattern following the pattern's solid cutting lines.

Step 2: Sew the kerchief

A: With the Wrong side of fabric facing up, fold over ¼ in/6 mm toward the kerchief's center on all sides, and press. Turn another ¼ in/6 mm around the entire kerchief and press again. Machine-stitch ³⁄₁₆ in/5 mm around the entire kerchief, making sure to sew through all layers of fabric, backstitching at the beginning and end. Press.

Simple Dress

This is a lovely, classic pinafore that is not very hard to make. I have made sure that little Miss Buttercup will have a comforting friend along with her at all times, attached on a string, hanging out in the pocket, ready to play whenever she wants to! Adding the pocket friend is optional (so is the pocket, for that matter). For this dress I recommend a cotton or linen fabric for the best fit.

Finished size:
17 in/43 cm long

Fabric:
1 yard (44 in wide) /90 cm (114 cm wide) cotton

Supplies:
Pattern from the front pocket of this book
Scissors
Straight pins
Fabric marker
Fadeout marker
Ruler
Iron
Thread
Pinking shears (optional)
4 in/10 cm thin round elastic or ribbon
1 small button
Hand-sewing needle
Cotton or polyester batting (optional)

Notes:
All seams are ½ in/12 mm unless otherwise noted. The seam allowance is included in the cutting instructions and pattern. Preshrink your fabric by washing, drying, and pressing it before you start.

Step 1: Cut out the pieces from the fabric

A: Cut out the pattern pieces provided at the front of this book.

B: Lay your fabric Right side up. Fold each selvedge edge to the center of the fabric; the selvedges will meet in the middle. Place the pattern pieces for the front of the dress on the fold as marked and pin them to the fabric. Cut out the dress piece by following the solid cutting lines on the pattern. To cut out the back of the dress repeat as above, but follow the solid cutting line (not the dotted fold line) on the pattern and place the pattern in the center of the folded-over fabric, not on the fold. Using your fabric marker, transfer the back neck opening mark to the Wrong side of the dress back fabric. Using your fadeout marker, transfer the pocket placement to the Right side of the front dress piece. [figure 2]

C: You will need three bias strips: two for the armholes and one for the neck. On the Wrong side of the fabric, at a 45-degree angle to the fabric's grain line, use your fabric marker to mark two strips that are 1½ in/3.8 cm wide x 14 in/36 cm long, and one strip that is 1½ in/3.8 cm wide x 17 in/43 cm long. Cut them out along your markings. (See figure 1 on page 24.)

D: With the Wrong side facing you, pin the pocket pattern piece to the fabric. Cut out the piece by following the solid cutting lines on the pattern.

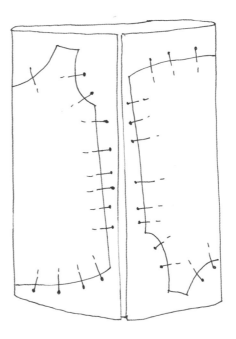

Figure 2

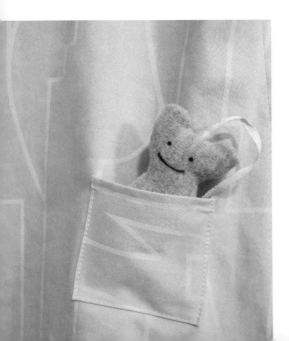

Step 2. Sew the dress together

A: Place the pocket piece Wrong side up. Fold over ¼ in/6 mm along the sides and bottom of the pocket, and press. Fold over ¼ in/6 mm along the pocket's top and press, then fold over ¼ in/6 mm again and press. Machine-stitch along the pocket top's folded-under edge, backstitching at the beginning and end.

B: Align the pocket piece with the placement marks on the fabric's Right side and pin it in place. Machine-stitch along the pocket's folded-under sides and bottom, backstitching at the beginning and end.

C: With the Right sides together, pin the dress's center back seam. Stitch from the hem to the opening mark, backstitching at the beginning and end. Trim the seam allowance to ¼ in/6 mm, up to the opening mark. Leave the seam allowance between the opening mark and neck at ½ in/12 mm and unstitched. Zigzag along each side of the seam allowance's edges to prevent fraying, being careful to not catch the straight seam in the zigzag. (If you are not able to zigzag, use pinking shears to trim the seam allowance to ¼ in/6 mm. This will help slow the fraying of the seams.) Press the seam open.

D: With the Wrong side facing you, press open ½ in/12 mm on each side of the unstitched seam allowance between the opening mark and neck on the back of the dress. Then turn the edges under ¼ in/6 mm of the seam allowance and press. Pin. Machine-stitch a seam around the opening, close to the fold, catching all the layers of the seam allowance you just pressed and backstitching at the beginning and end.

E: With the Right sides together, pin the dress's front and back together at the shoulder and side seams. Stitch across the shoulders and down each side seam, backstitching at the beginning and end. To prevent the seams from fraying, zigzag or use your pinking shears as in step C.

F: Fold under ½ in/12 mm at the short end of each of the 14 in/36 cm bias strips and press. Fold over and press ½ in/12 mm along one long side of each of the bias strips. With the Right sides together, and starting with the pressed-under end of the bias tape, pin the unfolded long side of the bias strip around one of the arm openings. Overlap the binding ¾ in/1.9 cm at the end and trim away the excess bias strip. Sew around the armhole, backstitching at the beginning and end of the seam. Trim the seam allowance to ¼ in/6 mm, and clip it around the curves, being careful not to clip through your seam. Repeat this step for the other armhole.

G: Fold under and press the binding inside the armhole. Pin the binding's folded edge to the inside of the dress, easing any wrinkles. You may need to smooth the binding with your fingers as you go to make it lie smoothly. Tuck the binding's raw end inside the folded end where the two ends meet so there are no raw edges. Machine-stitch closely to the folded edge of the binding, backstitching at the beginning and end of each seam. Repeat for the other arm opening.

H: Fold over and press ½ in/12 mm along one long side of the 17 in/43 cm bias strip. With the Right sides of the fabric together, pin the unfolded long side of the bias strip around the neck edge, matching raw edges and leaving ½ in/12 mm of the bias hanging off the edge at the center back opening. When you pin around entire neck, leave another ½ in/12 mm of the binding hanging off the center back opening. Stitch around the neck. Trim the seam allowance to ¼ in/6 mm and clip it around the curves. Do not trim off the ½ in/12 mm ends that are at the center back.

I: On the Wrong side of one end of the bias strip that is hanging over the center back opening, fold over ¼ in/6 mm and press. Fold over another ¼ in/6 mm and press. Repeat on the other side. Repeat step G for the neck, being sure to have the folded-under binding at the center back tucked just inside the center back opening so that it's not visible from the outside.

J: Cut a small loop of elastic or ribbon that will fit over your button, leaving ½ in/12 mm at each end for the seam allowance. At the top of the right-hand side of the center back opening, pin the elastic or ribbon loop inside the dress. If you're using ribbon, tuck the raw ends under so they are not visible. Using your hand-sewing needle and thread, securely tack the loop to the dress through the opening's seam allowance. Mark where the button should be placed opposite the loop and securely hand-stitch the button on the opposite side of the opening.

K: At the hem, fold over and press ½ in/12 mm. Then, fold over and press ½ in/12 mm again and pin. Machine-stitch along the folded edge, backstitching at the beginning and end of your seam.

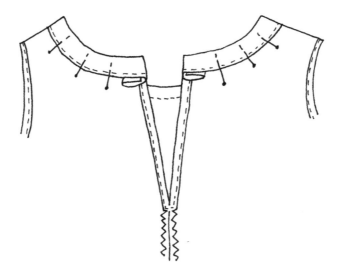

Figure 21

Step 3: Make the pocket friend (optional)

A: Using the pattern included in this book, trace the shape of the pocket friend on a piece of fabric. Repeat on a second piece of fabric.

B: Cut out the shapes.

C: Place the shapes together, with the Right sides facing each other.

D: Machine-stitch ¼ in/6 mm from the edge, backstitching at the beginning and end of your seam. Leave ¾ in/1.9 cm unstitched at the bottom.

E: Turn the friend Right side out. Stuff it with cotton or polyester batting.

F: Hand-sew the opening shut. Hand-sew cotton ribbon (approximately 5 in/13 cm) to the top of the friend's head, and sew the other end of the ribbon inside the pocket.

Simple Pants

There is nothing complicated here—simply pants with an elastic waistband. It couldn't be easier, and it couldn't be cuter. This is probably the most useful and practical garment I have made for my little boy, August. And do keep in mind that pants are for girls, too. If you feel extra adventurous and crafty, why don't you print your own fabric to use for these pants? Use the stencils I have provided at the back of this book, and follow the instructions on page 44.

Finished size:
8 in/20 cm inseam, 15½ in/39 cm outseam, 24 in/61 cm or smaller waist

Fabric:
¾ yard (44 in wide) /70 cm (114 cm wide) cotton

Supplies:
Pattern from the front pocket of this book
Scissors
Straight pins
Thread
Ruler
Pinking shears (optional)
Iron
Large safety pin
½ yard (½ in wide) /46 cm (12 mm wide) elastic

Notes:
All seams are ½ in/12 mm unless otherwise noted. The seam allowance is included in the cutting instructions and pattern. Preshrink your fabric by washing, drying, and pressing it before you start.

Step 1: Cut out the pieces from the fabric

A: Cut out the pattern piece provided at the front of this book.

B: Lay your fabric Right side up. Fold each selvedge edge to the center of the fabric; the selvedges will meet in the middle. Place the pattern on one fold, as marked, and pin the pattern piece to the fabric. Cut out the first piece of the pants following the solid cutting lines on the pattern. Repeat on the other fold for the second piece of the pants.

Step 2: Sew the pants together

A: Open up each piece of the pants and, with the Right sides together, place one on top of the other. Pin each side seam, and around the curved inseam.

B: Sew down each side seam, backstitching at the beginning and end. Sew the inseam, backstitching at the beginning and end. Trim the seam allowances to ¼ in/6 mm. Zigzag along the seam allowance's edge, being careful to not catch the straight seam in the zigzag. (If you are not able to zigzag, use pinking shears to trim the seam allowance to ¼ in/6 mm. This will help slow the fraying of the seams.) Press each seam.

C: With the Wrong side of fabric facing you, fold up ½ in/12 mm at the bottom of both legs and press. Then fold up another ½ in/12 mm and press. Pin along the folded edge. Machine-stitch close to the folded-under edge, backstitching at the beginning and end, making sure to stitch through all the layers of fabric.

D: With the Wrong side of fabric facing you, fold over ½ in/12 mm at the waist and press. Then fold over another ¾ in/1.9 cm and press. Leaving a 2 in/5 cm opening over one of the side seams, pin along the folded edge. Machine-stitch close to the folded-under edge, making sure to leave open the 2 in/5 cm over the side seam, and backstitching at the beginning and end of the seam.

E: Attach a large safety pin to one end of the elastic. Insert the safety pin into the 2 in/5 cm opening at the waist. Thread the elastic through the waistband by pushing the safety pin along and easing the fabric over the pin. The fabric will gather up over the pin, but just keep pushing it over the pin and inching forward, allowing the elastic to be pulled inside the waistband. Make sure to keep the other end of the elastic from being pulled inside the waistband. Once the pin emerges back out of the opening, pin the ends of the elastic together. Pull the elastic to the waist size of the child. Lay one end of elastic over the other and pin. Machine-stitch the elastic together and trim the excess.

F: Slip the elastic inside the waistband and pin the opening closed. Machine-stitch the opening closed, being careful to not stitch over the elastic, backstitching at the beginning and end.

Decorated Tees and Bodysuits

On the following pages I will show you some ideas for decorating your baby's shirts and other clothes. You can easily draw some airplanes—or write a manifesto—with fabric markers. Up for a challenge? Screen-print something cool on your baby's bunting. Want something simpler? Embellish a creeper with potato stamps.

At the back of this book are some stencils I've made for you to use. In the Resources section (page 140), I have listed places where you can buy T-shirts and bodysuits to create your masterpieces on. Now go do it ... and have fun!

Stencils

For some of the projects in this book I suggest stenciling. This is such an easy and fun printing technique. You can effortlessly decorate and customize your fabric projects with some dabs of ink.

In the back of this book I have included some stencils for you to use, but I recommend that you try making your own: It is much more satisfying.

It's easy to make your own stencil. Just transfer your design on to stiff paper or plastic, or you can use self-adhesive contact paper if you're printing on fabric. Cut the design out with scissors or a craft knife. Then, lay the template on top of the material you are going to stencil on, and pass the ink across the template with a hard brush or sponge. Special stencil brushes will work best, but any round, stiff-bristle brush will do the trick.

Stenciling works well on both the coarsest and finest of materials, but take care in creating your stencil design. You should avoid fine lines and delicate details, as they are difficult to cut and to print.

Please make sure to read the instructions on your ink jar or ink tube for heat setting the ink to the fabric. You don't want your sweet design to wash away.

Supplies:

Acetate, or stencil paper
Permanent marker
Craft knife
Cutting mat or heavy cardboard
Paints and inks for fabric
Old plate
Fabric
Masking tape
Stencil brush or sponge
Paper towels
Scrap paper
Scissors

Step 1: Make the stencil

A: Draw your design onto the acetate or stencil paper with a permanent marker.

B: Using a craft knife and cutting mat or heavy cardboard, cut out your design, making sure to leave ample room around the motif to protect the fabric from accidental splashes. You will need to cut a separate stencil for each color used in the design.

Step 2: Print on the fabric

A: Pour a small amount of paint on to an old plate.

B: Place your stencil on top of your fabric. Secure the stencil to the material using masking tape so it will not move while you're printing. (This is why using self-adhesive plastic as a stencil is so handy; you don't need to secure the stencil with masking tape.)

C: Using a stencil brush or sponge, dab an even amount of ink through the stencil. Applying several thin layers of ink yields a better result than using too much ink at one time.

D: If you are printing more than one color, finish with the first before moving on to the next one. Let the ink dry before changing stencils. It is easiest if you have a separate brush or sponge for each color.

Potato prints

You might remember printing with potatoes when you were a little kid yourself—and wasn't it fun? This is an easy, effective, and inexpensive method for printing on fabric, and you can get some surprisingly nice results. Just remember to keep the designs simple.

For cutting out the design, you can use a paring knife, pumpkin-carving tools, or linoleum- or wood-cutting tools.

Supplies:

Potatoes
Cutting tools
Paper towels
Pencil or black marker
Paint, gouache, or fabric paint
Stamp pad (optional)
Paintbrushes or sponges
Fabric
Scrap paper

Step 1: Prepare the stamp

A: Cut a potato in half. Blot the cut surface with paper towels to absorb as much moisture as possible.

B: Draw your motif on the potato with a pencil or marker.

C: Using your knife or cutting tool, carve around the outline of your design. Cut away the background to a depth of about ¼ in/6 mm.

Step 2: Print on the fabric

A: Apply ink or paint to the potato stamp with a brush or a sponge, or use a stamp pad.

B: Gently press the painted surface onto your fabric and press evenly, transferring the image to your material.

Notes:
You can use various kinds of printing/fabric ink: Make sure that you get paint or ink made for fabric if you'll be printing on clothing. The paint should be thick, not watery, for a bold, sharp print.

Any variety of potato will do, but large baking potatoes are best. You can make two stamps from each potato.
You can easily reuse the potato to print for different colors. Carefully wash the ink off your potato with running water, and blot it with a paper towel. Set the potato aside and let it dry before stamping. If details on the potato get clogged with paint, gently rinse the stamp or wipe it with paper towels.

A potato stamp has a life span of a day or two (you can store the washed potato stamp in a plastic bag overnight).

Baby Hat

My son, August, was born in the middle of
January and, boy, would we bundle him up to
protect him from Brooklyn's icy weather! I was
particularly concerned about his tiny ears—
I wanted so much to protect them and make
sure that he did not get an earache. This soft
hat did the trick. August was not only protected
properly, he was super-cute in it!

Finished size:
17 in/43 cm circumference (when not stretched out) x 10 in/25 cm tall

Fabric:
½ yard (44 in wide) /46 cm (114 cm wide) soft, stretchy fabric, such as microfleece
20 in/50 cm ribbon

Supplies:
Pattern from the front pocket of this book
Scissors
Straight pins
Thread
Point turner
Hand-sewing needle

Notes:
All seams are ½ in/12 mm unless otherwise noted. The seam
allowance is included in the cutting instructions and pattern.
Preshrink your fabric by washing, drying, and pressing it
before you start.

Step 1: Cut out the pieces from the fabric

A: Cut out the pattern piece provided at the front of this book.

B: Fold your fabric Right sides together, selvedges aligned. Pin the pattern piece to the fabric, aligning the grain line on the pattern with the grain of the fabric, and making sure to leave room to cut another set. Cut out one set of hat pieces following the solid cutting lines on the pattern. Then re-pin the pattern to the fabric and cut out the second set, also following the solid cutting lines.

C: Cut the ribbon into 2 pieces, each 10 in/25 cm long.

Step 2: Sew the hat together

A: With the Right sides together, pin each set of hat pieces together along the side seams. On one set leave a 2 in/5 cm opening near the top.

B: Sew down each set's pinned sides, backstitching at the beginning and end of each seam. Be sure to leave the 2 in/5 cm opening on one of the sets. Trim the seam allowance to ¼ in/6 mm, but do not trim the seam allowance at the 2 in/5 cm opening, and clip the curved edges (be careful not to clip through the seam).

C: Press the seams open. Turn one set Right side out and gently push the top nub of the hat out with the point turner.

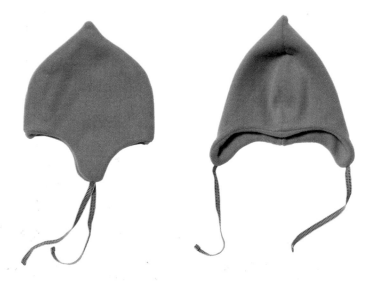

D: Insert the Right-side-out layer inside the Wrong-side-out layer, so that the Right sides of the layers are facing each other. Pin them together. [figure 4]

E: Tie a knot on one end of each piece of ribbon. Insert one ribbon piece in the center curve of each earflap, with the length of the ribbon sandwiched between the Right sides of the fabric and the knotted ends aligned with the fabric's raw edges. Pin around the raw edges. Sew along the pinned edge, backstitching at the beginning and end. Sew a second seam over the ribbon ends to secure them. Trim the seam allowance to ¼ in/6 mm, and clip the curved edges (be careful not to clip through the seam). [figure 5]

F: Turn the hat Right side out through the 2 in/5 cm opening. Use your finger to smooth the curves, edges, and earflaps.

G: Fold the opening's seam allowance in by ½ in/12 mm and press. Slipstitch the opening closed by hand. Tuck the layer with the opening inside the other layer and press the bottom seam flat. [figure 6]

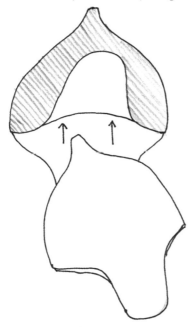

Figure 4

Figure 5

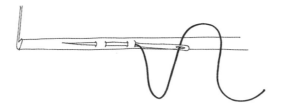

Figure 6

Soft Hat and Scarf

Made with the softest of fleeces, this smart set will keep your little bambino or bambina warm, happy, and adorable. The hat is basically a square—you can tie off the corners with embroidery string to give the hat ears, if you want. The scarf can be decorated with a button. It's up to you!

Safety note:
Because of potential choking hazards, this scarf is meant for older babies.

Hat

Finished size:
19 in/48 cm circumference (will stretch, depending on your fabric) x 9 in/23 cm tall

Fabric:
¾ yard (44 in wide) /70 cm (114 cm wide) stretchy soft fabric, such as cotton fleece or microfleece
8 in/20 cm embroidery floss, string, or ribbon to tie the ears (optional)

Supplies:
Ruler
Fabric marker
Scissors
Straight pins
Thread
Iron
Point turner
Hand-sewing needle

Notes:
All seams are ½ in/12 mm unless otherwise noted. The seam allowance is included in the cutting instructions. Preshrink your fabric by washing, drying, and pressing it before you start.

Step 1: Cut out the pieces from the fabric

A: Fold your fabric Right sides together, selvedges aligned. Measure and mark two pieces, each 9½ in/24 cm wide on the fold x 9 in/23 cm long, directly onto the Wrong side of fabric, using your ruler and fabric marker. Cut out each piece on the fold, following the marked lines. [figure 7]

Step 2: Sew the hat together

A: On one rectangle, with the fabric still folded and the Right sides together, pin both 9 in/23 cm edges together. Leave a 2 in/5 cm opening in the seam on one side, near the folded edge. Sew the pinned edges, backstitching at the beginning and end of each seam. Be sure to leave open the 2 in/5 cm opening on one side. Trim the seam allowance to ¼ in/6 mm, and clip the corners near the fold at a 45-degree angle. Do not trim the seam allowance at the 2 in/5 cm opening.

B: Repeat with the second rectangle, but this time do not leave the 2 in/5 cm opening.

C: Press open the seams of both rectangles. Turn one layer Right side out, and push out the corners with your point turner so they are square.

D: Insert the Right side out layer inside the other rectangle, so that Right sides of the layers are facing each other. Pin the unstitched edges together, then sew along them. Trim the seam allowance to ¼ in/6 mm.

E: Pull the hat Right side out through the 2 in/5 cm opening. Fold the seam allowance of the opening under by ½ in/12 mm and press. Slipstitch the opening closed by hand. Turn the hat Right side out (so the seam you just hand-sewed is on the inside).

Step 3: Make the ears (optional)

A: Cut the embroidery floss, string, or ribbon into two 4 in/10 cm pieces. Pinch 2 in/5 cm down from the top corner of each hat and tie a piece of string or ribbon tightly around the pinch to make the ears. Make sure the knot is secure.

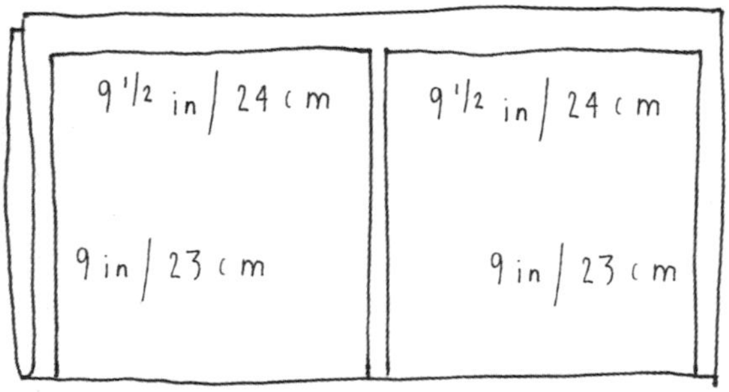

Figure 7

Scarf

Finished size:
25 in/64 cm long x 4 in/10 cm wide

Fabric:
⅓ yard (44 in wide) /30 cm (114 cm wide) stretchy soft fabric, such as a microfleece.

Supplies:
Ruler
Fabric marker
Scissors
Straight pins
Thread
Point turner
Iron
Hand-sewing needle
1 button (optional)

Notes:
All seams are ½ in/12 mm unless otherwise noted. The seam
allowance is included in the cutting instructions. Preshrink
your fabric by washing, drying, and pressing it before you start.

Step 1: Cut out the pieces from the fabric

A: Fold the fabric in half, Right sides together, selvedges aligned. Measure and mark two pieces, each 5 in/13 cm wide (on the fold) x 13 in/33 cm long, directly on to the Wrong side of the fabric, using a ruler and fabric marker. Cut out each piece on the fold following the marked lines.

B: Fold the pieces in half lengthwide, Right sides together. Cut the corners on one end at long angles, as shown. [figure 8]

Step 2: Sew the scarf

A: With the Right sides together, pin the two pieces together leaving a 3 in/8 cm opening in the middle of one of the long sides. Stitch around the entire scarf, being sure to leave the opening unstitched and backstitching at the beginning and end. Trim the seam allowance to ¼ in/6 mm, but do not trim the seam allowance at the 3 in/8 cm opening. Clip the corners at a 45-degree angle.

B: Turn the scarf Right side out through the 3 in/8 cm opening. Push out the corners using your point turner. Press the seams.

C: Fold the opening's seam allowance under by ½ in/12 mm and pin it in place. Slipstitch the opening closed by hand.

D: Fold the scarf's angled end over by 4 in/10 cm and pin it in place.

E: Center the button, if using, in the pointy end, about 1 in/2.5 cm from the scarf's tip. Sew the button down very securely. If not using button, sew the pointy end of scarf down, close to the edge, backstitch at each end.

Figure 8

Soft Rattle

Babies love rattles. I don't know why—they simply do. (Cats take to them as well, so watch out!) This little friend will fit perfectly in your baby's hand. It is best made out of terry cloth, stretchy soft cotton, or microfleece. Do keep in mind that this toy will end up in your baby's mouth, so don't pick a linty fabric. You can add a little bell in the rattle while stuffing it with batting, or you can leave it out and make it a silent friend. The eyes, nose, and mouth can be embroidered on, or you can draw them with a fabric pen. The ears can be made smaller or longer, depending on the length of your ribbon.

Finished size:
8 in/20 cm x 2 in/5 cm

Fabric:
¼ yard (44 in wide) /23 cm (114 cm wide) cotton
4 in/10 cm (or more) ribbon

Supplies:
Pattern from the front pocket of this book
Scissors
Straight pins
Dressmaker's tracing paper
Tracing wheel
Fabric marker
Embroidery floss
Hand-sewing needle
Thread
Fiberfil or stuffing
Small bell (optional)

Notes:
All seams are ½ in/12 mm unless otherwise noted. The seam allowance is included in the cutting instructions and pattern. Preshrink your fabric by washing, drying, and pressing it before you start.

Step 1: Cut out the pieces from the fabric

A: Cut out the pattern piece provided at the front of this book.

B: Fold your fabric Right sides together. Pin the pattern piece to the fabric. Cut out the rattle following the solid cutting lines on the pattern. Place the fabric and pattern on top of your tracing paper and, using your tracing wheel, trace around the stitching lines on the pattern, transferring the stitching lines to the fabric's Wrong side. Repeat on the Wrong side of the other piece of fabric. Use your fabric marker to transfer the eye and the placement marks for the ears to the Right side of the fabric on both pieces.

C: Cut the ribbon into two pieces, each at least 2 in/5 cm long.

Step 2: Embroider the eyes

A: Pull about 4 strands of embroidery floss from the strand, and thread your hand-sewing needle. Make a knot at the end of the floss. Take one side of the rattle and, with the Right side facing you, hold the eye area taut between your fingers. Embroider the eye with a straight stitch, filling in the circle. Repeat on other piece of rattle. Set aside the unused floss.

Step 3: Sew the rattle

A: Pin the pieces Right sides together, leaving the bottom of the rattle open. Fold each piece of ribbon in half and, matching them up with the placement marks, sandwich them between the two fabric layers. The raw edge of the ribbon should align with the raw edge of the fabric, with the folded edge hidden inside. Machine-stitch around the rattle following the stitching line you transferred to the fabric, paying close attention to the tight curves, catching the ears in the seam, and backstitching at the beginning and end. Be sure not to sew closed the bottom of the rattle. Trim the seam allowance to ¼ in/6 mm and clip along the curves, being careful not to clip though your seam.

B: Turn the rattle Right side out through the opening, smoothing the curves with your fingers as you go. Press. Stuff the rattle with the Fiberfil and bell, if using. You may need to use your finger or the eraser end of a pencil to get the stuffing into the rattle's nose.

C: When the rattle is stuffed to the fullness you like, fold under the opening's seam allowance by ½ in/12 mm. Pin it shut and, using your hand-sewing needle and regular thread, slipstitch the opening closed.

Step 4: Embroider the nose

A: Using your needle threaded with embroidery floss, embroider a small nose at the tip of the face of the rattle using a straight stitch.

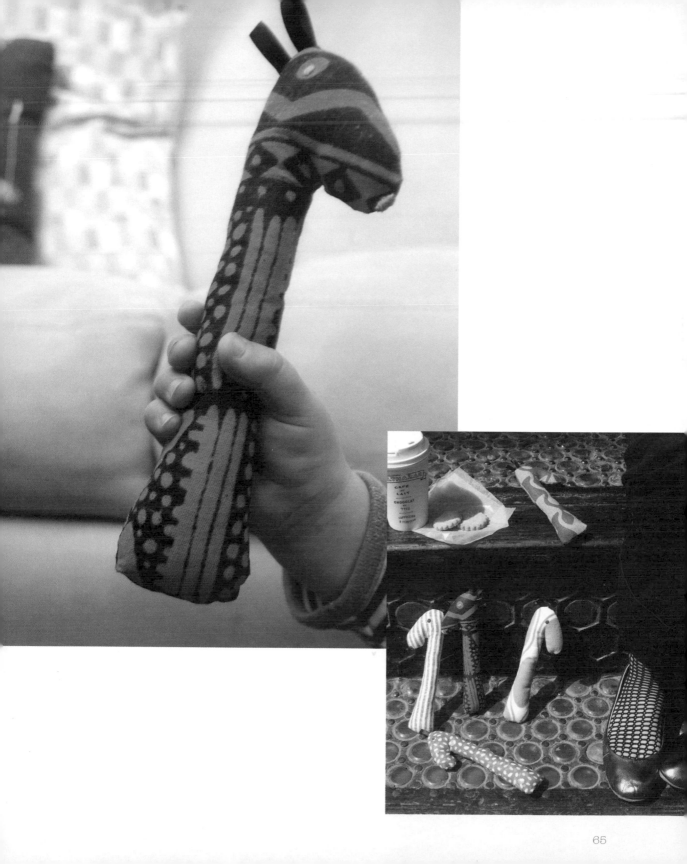

Buddy

Here's a huggable buddy for your wee one. There is Velcro on each of Buddy's hands to give him extra hugging power. These guys can be made in various sizes—the bigger the better, I think. There's not a pattern for these guys, just my drawings of suggested shapes, which you'll find on page 71.

I recommend a soft fabric, such as flannel, to make him extra huggable. Stencil a face on him (I have included some at the back of this book) to give him some personality. You will have to maneuver carefully when you sew the buddy up, as there are a lot of arms and legs to keep track of. But persevere—it's worth it!

Finished size:
Up to you, but the big buddy in this book has a body that's 23 in/58 cm x 14 in/36 cm, plus long arms and legs

Fabric:
1½ yards (44 in wide) /1.4 m (114 cm wide) medium weight cotton

Supplies:
Ruler
Fabric marker
Scissors
3 in (1 in wide) /8 cm (2.5 cm wide) strip Velcro
Thread
Straight pins
Point turner
Iron
1 bag Fiberfil or stuffing
Hand-sewing needle

Notes:
All seams are ½ in/12 mm unless otherwise noted. The seam allowance is included in the cutting instructions. Preshrink your fabric by washing, drying, and pressing it before you start.

Step 1: Cut out the pieces from the fabric

A: Fold your fabric in half, Right sides together, with selvedges aligned. Measure and mark the dimensions below directly on to the Wrong side of fabric, using your ruler and fabric marker. Cut out each piece following the marked lines.

For the body, cut:
2 rounded-off rectangles, 24 in/61 cm long x 15 in/38 cm wide. Curve the tops a bit more than the bottoms.
For the arms, cut:
4 rectangles, wider at one end than the other, 17 in/43 cm long x 4 in/10 cm wide at one end and 3 in/8 cm wide at the other.
For the legs, cut:
4 rectangles, wider at one end than the other, 21 in/53 cm long x 4 in/10 cm wide at one end and 3 in/8 cm wide at the other.

Step 2: Sew the buddy

A: Take one half of the Velcro and center it on the Right side of the wide end of one arm piece. The Velcro should run lengthwise up the arm, 1 in/2.5 cm from the bottom edge (imagine it's on the back of the buddy's hand), and centered between the long edges. Machine-stitch around all sides of the Velcro, being sure to backstitch at the beginning and end. Repeat with the other side of the Velcro on another arm piece (this one goes on the buddy's palm).

B: With the Right sides together, pin the arm pieces together and the leg pieces together. Leave the narrow ends of them open and unpinned. Make sure that each arm has one piece of Velcro—you don't want both Velcro pieces on one arm! Stitch around the three pinned sides of the arms and legs, being sure to backstitch at the beginning and end. Trim the seam allowances to ¼ in/6 mm and clip the corners to a 45-degree angle. Turn them Right side out through the open ends. Use your point turner to poke out the corners. Press.

C: Stuff the legs and arms with the Fiberfil. They should be full and soft, not overstuffed. Leave the last 1 in/2.5 cm by the opening unstuffed. Machine-baste the openings closed 1 in/2.5 cm from the raw edge.

D: With the Right sides facing each other, pin the top of the body pieces together. Velcro the arms together, then sandwich them between the body pieces with their raw edges aligned with the body's raw edges and roughly at the top ⅓ of the body. Pin them securely in place. Keep pinning down the sides of the body until you get to the bottom corners. Sandwich the legs between the body pieces, centering them at the bottom of the body, with the raw edges aligned. Pin them securely in place. Because the body will be lumpy with all of the legs and arms inside, you'll need to make sure that the body's seams are all aligned and pinned securely before sewing.

E: Stitch around the body, leaving a 5 in/12 cm opening along one side below an arm and backstitching at the beginning and end. Leave the opening seam allowance untrimmed, but trim the rest of the seam allowance to ¼ in/6 mm and clip the corners to a 45-degree angle (be careful not to clip through the seam).

F: Turn the buddy Right side out through the opening. Stuff the body until it's plump and not too overstuffed.

G: Fold under ½ in/12 mm on each side of the opening and pin it closed. Slipstitch the opening closed by hand.

H : Stencil the face onto the front of the buddy (see page 44).

Soft Letters

These letters are easy to make: Just cut out the letters you want in cotton, canvas, or craft felt, then finish the edge off with pinking shears or a zigzag stitch. If you are lucky enough to own an overlocker, you would of course use that, but it is not a must. Should you want to take this project further, I encourage a little bit of surface decoration. How about some embroidery stitches, a stencil print, or fabric marker doodles? You could make the whole alphabet and help your wee one to get a head start in spelling, or you could make the letters for your little one's name—whatever suits your fancy.

Fabric:
¼ in/23 cm yard felt or nonfraying fabric, or two felt squares per letter

Supplies:
Pencil with eraser
Photocopier
Fadeout marker
Scissors
Straight pins
Ruler
Thread
Fiberfil or cotton stuffing
Pinking shears

Notes:
All seams are ½ in/12 mm unless otherwise noted. The seam allowance is included in the cutting instructions and pattern. Preshrink your fabric by washing, drying, and pressing it before you start.

Step 1: Cut out the letters

A: Draw the letters you would like to use.

Then, using a photocopier, enlarge the letters to a size you would like to use and outline the letter shapes on your felt or fabric using your fadeout marker.

B: Cut out the enlarged letters ("pattern pieces") that you created.

Repeat on the other piece of felt or fabric to cut two of each letter.

Step 2: Sew the letters

A: Pin the two letter pieces together, leaving a 2 in/5 cm opening along one edge. Carefully stitch around the letter, making sure to leave open the 2 in/5 cm opening, and backstitching at the beginning and end. Trim the seam allowance to ⅛ in/3 mm, but do not trim the opening's seam allowance yet.

B: Stuff your letter with the Fiberfil or cotton stuffing. You may need to use the eraser end of a pencil to help you get the stuffing inside the tight corners of some of the letters.

C: Pin the opening closed, and machine-stitch the opening closed following the original seam allowance. Trim the seam allowance with pinking shears to ⅛ in/3 mm.

Soft Book

When you're out and about with your little one, there will be many times when you'll be glad you brought along a toy. This soft book will pack easily in any bag, and it hardly weighs a thing. By using felt, which doesn't unravel, you can simply cut out your pages and not worry about finishing the edges. You can trim the edges with pinking shears if you want, to add to the cuteness, but that's not at all necessary. Decorate the pages with stencil prints from the back of this book, fabric markers, embroidery— or a combination of all those techniques.

Finished size:
6 in/15 cm x 6 in/15 cm

Fabric:
You need 2 felt squares, each at least 12 in/30 cm x 12 in/30 cm
You can use the precut felt squares available in most craft and art stores.

Supplies:
Ruler
Scissors
Stencil supplies (see page 45)
Pins
Embroidery thread
Embroidery needle

Notes:
I recommend that you decorate your pages before stitching them together. For instructions on stenciling patterns and motifs, see page 44.

Step 1: Cut out the pieces from the fabric

A: From the felt, cut three pieces, each 12 in/30 cm x 6 in/15 cm.

Step 2: Decorate the pages

A: Turn to page 44 for directions on how to stencil.

Step 3: Sew the book together

A: Fold each piece in half. Stack the three pieces on top of each other.

B: Pin the pages together to prevent them from shifting while you bind them.

C: Using embroidery thread and a needle, sew a blanket stitch along the spine of the book. Make sure to secure the thread at the end. [figure 9]

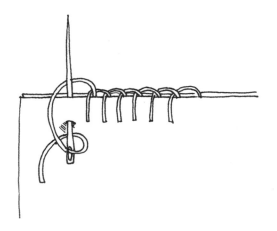

Figure 9

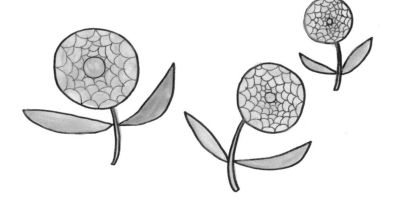

Tag Blankie

This is one of those items I just marvel at—a tag blankie! Now, how did anybody come up with that? It is a rather brilliant item, since it seems that babies love to suck on shiny ribbon tags. The instructions are easy to follow, and you can make it any size you want. It is really fun to plan this piece; just think about all the combinations you can create using various colored and patterned ribbons.

Finished size:
12 in/30 cm x 12 in/30 cm

Fabric:
½ yard (44 in wide) /46 cm (114 cm wide) lightweight cotton
16 pieces of various ribbons, 4 in/10 cm to 8 in/20 cm long

Supplies:
Ruler
Fabric marker
Scissors
Straight pins
Thread
Point turner

Notes:
All seams are ½ in/12 mm unless otherwise noted. The seam
allowance is included in the cutting instructions. Preshrink
your fabric by washing, drying, and pressing it before you start.

Step 1: Cut out the pieces from the fabric

A: Measure and mark two 13 in/33 cm x 13 in/33 cm pieces directly onto the Wrong side of the cotton fabric, using your ruler and fabric marker. Cut out each piece following the marked lines.

Step 2: Sew the tag blankie

A: Place the fabric pieces Right sides together. Fold the ribbon pieces in half. Starting on one side, sandwich the ribbons between the two fabric pieces with the folded edge inside the fabric and raw edges aligned with the raw edges of the fabric. Space them evenly along the edges, varying the colors, lengths, and types of ribbons. Pin the ribbons in place through both layers of fabric as you go. Repeat on all sides of the blankie. Leave a 3 in/8 cm opening on one side.

B: Machine-stitch around the entire square, securing the ribbons in the seam as you go. Backstitch at the beginning and end, and be sure to leave the 3 in/8 cm open. Trim the seam allowances to ¼ in/6 mm, and clip the corners at a 45-degree angle close to the corner. Do not trim the seam allowance at the opening.

C: Turn the blankie Right side out. Use the point turner to poke out the corners. Fold under the ½ in/12 mm seam allowance on the top and bottom of the opening, press it, and pin it closed. Press the entire circumference of the blankie.

D: Pin around the edge of the blankie. Machine-stitch a ¼ in/6 mm seam around the edge of the blankie, being sure to close the 3 in/8 cm opening. Backstitch at the beginning and end.

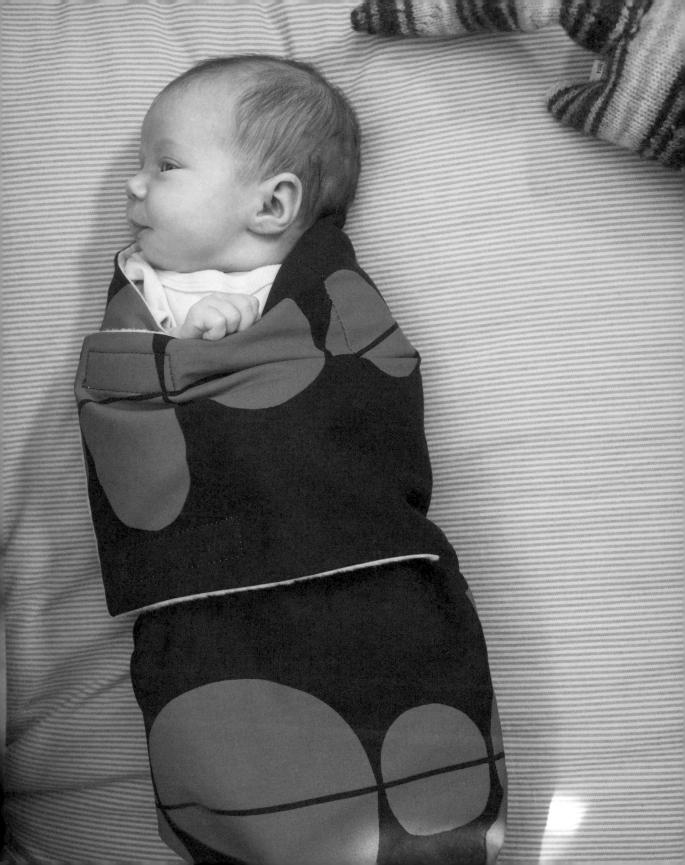

Snuggler

One of the first things a new parent will learn is how to swaddle the little one. It's a great comforting technique that really works. Our son, August, would always calm down when we rolled him up like a little burrito.

I received a super cozy bundler as a gift, and I simply loved it. I could wrap August up in a jiffy and we would all be much happier. I've made a few modifications to this snuggler design, but it's still very similier to the one I had originally received. It makes a great present at a baby shower.

Finished size:
20 in/51 cm long x 11 in/28 cm wide, plus the wraps

Fabric:
1 yard (44 in wide) /90 cm (114 cm wide) medium weight cotton
1 yard (44 in wide) /90 cm (114 cm wide) soft fabric, such as microfleece

Supplies:
Pattern from the front pocket of this book
Scissors
Straight pins
Fadeout marker
½ yard (1 in wide) /46 cm (2.5 cm wide) Velcro
Iron
Thread
Point turner
Hand-sewing needle

Notes:
All seams are ½ in/12 mm unless otherwise noted. The seam allowance is included in the cutting instructions and pattern. Preshrink your fabric by washing, drying, and pressing it before you start.

Step 1: Cut out the pieces from the fabric

A: Cut out the pattern pieces provided at the front of this book.

B: Fold the cotton fabric Right sides together, selvedges aligned. Pin the pattern pieces to the fabric, aligning the fold marks with the fold of the fabric. Cut out each piece following the solid cutting lines on the pattern. Before you remove the pattern, transfer the darts and other placement marks to the Wrong side of the fabric on both sides of the fold on each piece.

C: Repeat step B with the fleece.

D: Using your fadeout marker on the Right side of the cotton fabric, place the pattern on the large fabric piece and transfer the Velcro placement marks that are labeled "A". Then, on the Right side of the large fleece piece, transfer the Velcro placement marks that are labeled "B".

Step 2: Sew the snuggler

A: Starting with the darts, on the large cotton piece, with the Right sides together, fold over the fabric so that a fold runs down the center of the dart triangle and both straight marked lines match up. Pin. Repeat for all the darts on both pieces of fabric. Machine-stitch from the raw edge of the fabric to the end of the darts, backstitching at the beginning and end. You should sew all the way to the fold at dart's end. Trim the seam allowances to ¼ in/6 mm, clipping open the fold to lay flat, and press open. Repeat on the fleece pieces. [figure 10]

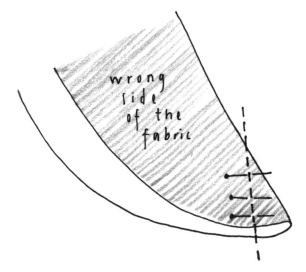

Figure 10

B: With the cotton piece's Right sides together, place the bottom of the snuggler on the larger top piece. Pin. Make sure it's aligned perfectly with the placement marks around the bottom curve and edges. Repeat with the fleece pieces. Machine-stitch from the placement mark on one side around the curve to the mark on the other side, backstitching at the beginning and end. Repeat with the fleece pieces. Trim the seam allowance to ¼ in/6 mm up to the placement marks, and clip around the curved edges (be careful not to cut through the seam). Press the seams open. [figure 11]

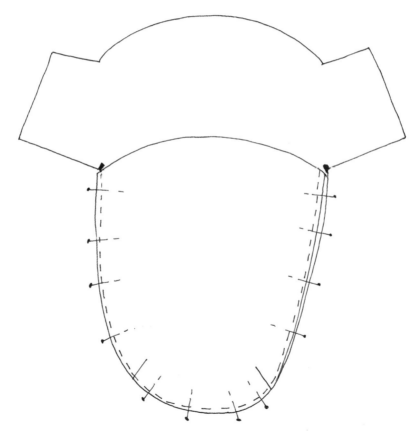

Figure 11

C: Turn the cotton layer Right side out, and leave the fleece layer Wrong side out. Insert the cotton layer inside the fleece layer, so that the Right sides of the layers are facing each other, tucking the pouch part down inside the snuggler and aligning the flaps and edges. Pin around the back, flaps, and top of the pouch. Leave a 3 in/8 cm opening under one of the flaps. Stitch along the pinned edge, being sure to leave the opening unstitched and backstitching at the beginning and end. Ease your way around the corners where the pouch meets the top of the snuggler. Trim the seam allowance to ¼ in/6 mm, except at the 3 in/8 cm opening on one of the flaps. Clip the curved edges, being careful not to clip through the seam. Clip the corners at a 45-degree angle. Turn the snuggler Right side out through the opening, smoothing the curved parts with your fingers and using your point turner to poke out the corners. Tuck the fleece pouch layer inside the cotton layer. The fleece should be the inside of the snuggler.

D: Fold the ½ in/12 mm seam allowance on both sides of the opening inside. Press and pin. Slipstitch the opening closed by hand.

E: On the cotton layer, pin the prickly side of the Velcro pieces, aligning with the placement marks. Machine-stitch around each side of the Velcro, backstitching at the beginning and end.

F: On the fleece layer, pin the soft side of the Velcro pieces, aligning with the placement marks. Machine-stitch around each side of the Velcro, backstitching at the beginning and end.

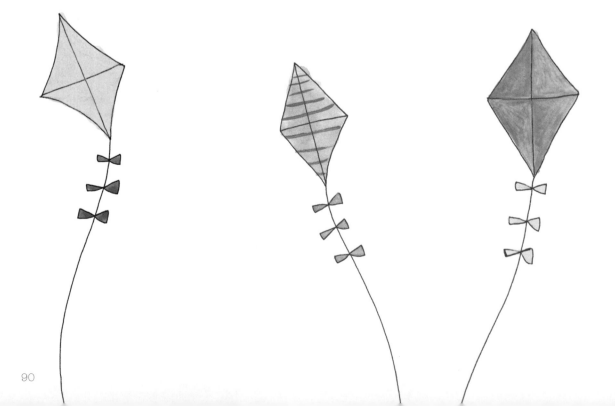

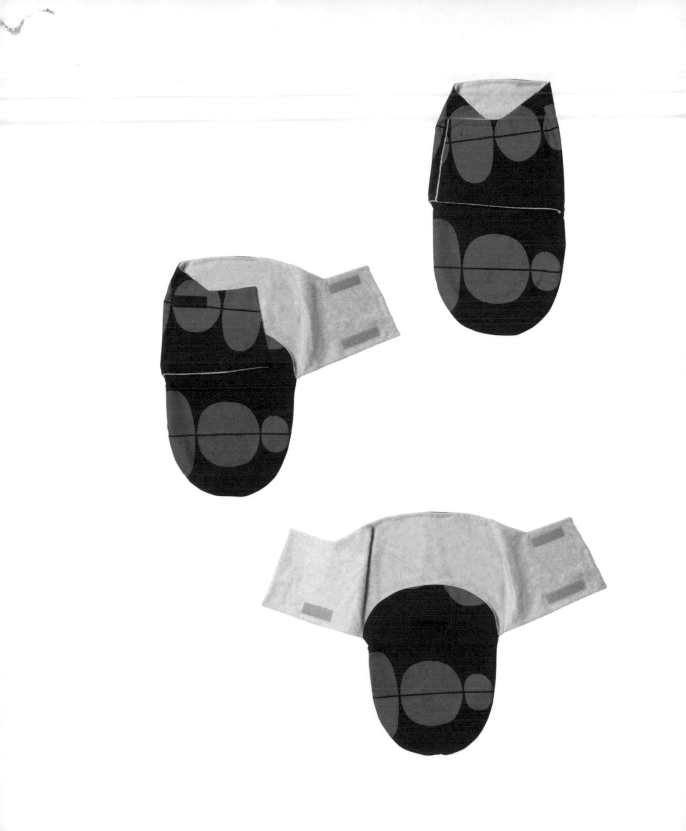

Bib

Now, here's a classic gift to give and receive. Bibs can be so darn cute! A functional bib would have a tray attached to it to catch all of that goop that missed the mouth (and that would be a lot of goop). The closest I can come to that is this bib made from plastic laminated fabric or oilcloth. The bib's pocket will capture some of that stray food before it lands on the floor.

This is a remarkably easy bib to make. Just take a couple of turns using a zigzag seam or an overlocker and soon you can give those bibs out left and right!

Finished size:
7½ in/19 cm tall x 9 in/23 cm wide, plus neck piece

Fabric:
½ yard (44 in wide) /46 cm (114 cm wide) laminated cotton or oilcloth

Supplies:
Pattern from the front pocket of this book
Scissors
Straight pins
Fadeout marker
1½ in (½ in wide) /3.9 cm (12 mm wide) Velcro

Step 1: Cut out the pieces from the fabric

A: Cut out the pattern pieces provided at the front of this book.

B: Pin the pattern pieces to the Wrong side of the fabric. Align the grain line on the pattern with the grain line of the fabric. Cut out each piece following the solid cutting lines on the pattern.

C: Using your fadeout marker, copy the pocket placement marks on the large pattern piece to the Right side of the large piece of fabric. Copy the Velcro placement on the short tip of the neck to the Right side of the fabric. On the Wrong side of the fabric, copy the Velcro placement to the long tip of the neck.

Step 2: Sew the bib

A: Zigzag tightly along the straight edge of the pocket.

B: With the Right side of the large bib piece facing you, place the pocket piece Right side up along the bottom of the bib, aligning the bottom edges. Pin. Machine-baste the pocket to the bib along the curved edge using a ¼ in/6 mm seam.

C: Zigzag tightly around the entire outer edge of the bib, taking your time on the tighter curves. Be sure to secure both the bib and the pocket. Backstitch at the beginning and end.

D: Align the prickly side of the Velcro with the marks you made on the Right side of the fabric on the short tip of the neck. Pin in place. Machine-stitch around the entire edge of the Velcro. Align the soft side of the Velcro with the marks you made on the Wrong side of the neck's long tip. Pin in place. Machine-stitch around the entire edge of the Velcro.

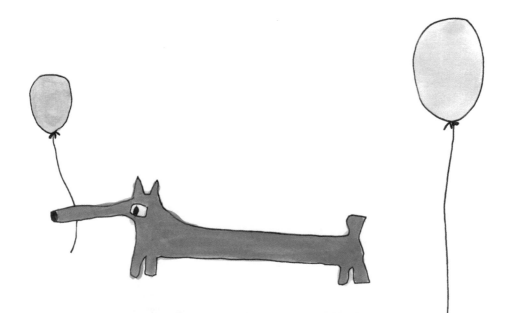

Play Quilt with Pocket

Mom and Dad will spend a whole lot of time on the floor from now on, and so will Baby. I quickly learned that the little nipper makes all kinds of stains while hanging out on the floor. I really was not ready to invest in a new rug, so I made a blanket instead. It is big enough for my son, August, and his toys, but also small enough to easily fit in the washer (this item will get washed a gazillion times). I added a little pocket for a toy or a wipe.

Finished size:

28 in/71 cm x 33 in/84 cm

Fabric:

Cotton squares and rectangles of various colors and patterns. On one piece you'll see both the Right and Wrong sides, so pick one that you like both sides of.

1 yard (44 in wide) /90 cm (114 cm wide) medium to heavy cotton, twill, or canvas for the back of the quilt

1 yard/90 cm medium-thickness quilting batting

Supplies:

Ruler
Fabric marker
Scissors
Iron
Thread
Straight pins
Point turner
Hand-sewing needle
Embroidery floss (optional)

I encourage you to make up your own sizes of quilting squares (but you do have to make sure that they are 8 in/20 cm wide). Just cut out some pieces in your favorite cottons and sew them together, keeping in mind that the final panel size should end up being 8 in/20 cm x 34 in/86 cm. You need to make four of these panels. The four panels will then be sewn together. Be sure to read the instructions to figure out how to make the pocket before you get started on the quilt top.

Notes:
All seams are ½ in/12 mm unless otherwise noted. The seam allowance is included in the cutting instructions.
Preshrink your fabric by washing, drying, and pressing it before you start.

Step 1: Cut out the pieces from the fabric

A: Measure and mark the dimensions directly on to the Wrong side of fabric, using your ruler and fabric marker. Cut out each piece following the marked lines.

From the cotton: Cut as many pieces as needed: squares and rectangles 8 in/20 cm wide x a variety of lengths. One of the rectangles should be 8 in/20 cm wide x 16 in/41 cm long; this will be the pocket piece in one corner of the quilt.

From the heavy fabric: Cut 1 piece: 29 in/74 cm long x 34 in/86 cm wide

From the batting: Cut 1 rectangle: 29 in/74 cm long x 34 in/86 cm wide

Step 2: Sew the quilt

A: With the Wrong side facing you on the 8 in/20 cm x 16 in/41 cm rectangle, fold over ½ in/12 mm along the 8 in/20 cm side and press. Fold over ½ in/12 mm again and press. Machine-stitch a seam along the folded edge, backstitching at the beginning and end. With the Right side facing you, fold up the hemmed edge 6 in/15 cm and pin along the side seams. Baste along the side seams a ¼ in/6 mm seam from the fold to the hemmed edge. This is your pocket piece.

B: Piece together the cotton squares and rectangles, Right sides together, so that you end up with four strips that are 8 in/20 cm wide x at least 34 in/86 cm long. Make sure that the pocket piece is at the end of one strip, with the folded edge at the bottom of the strip. Machine-stitch across each 8 in/20 cm pieced seam. Trim the seam allowances to ¼ in/6 mm and press open. Trim each strip's length to 34 in/86 cm. [figure 12]

C: With the Right sides together, pin one strip to the other along the long edge. Machine-stitch along the pinned edge, backstitching at the beginning and end. Repeat with the other strips, saving the strip with the pocket for last. You should now have all 4 strips sewn together with the pocket at one corner. Trim the seam allowances to ¼ in/6 mm and press open.

D: With the Wrong side of the heavy fabric facing up, lay the batting on top of the fabric. Pin around the edges. Baste ¼ in/6 mm from the edge around the entire rectangle.

E: With the Right sides of the heavy fabric and pieced cotton facing each other and the batting on the outside, pin the pieced cotton to the fabric backing, leaving a 6 in/15 cm opening on one side. Machine-stitch around the entire quilt, making sure to leave the opening unstitched, and backstitching at the beginning and end of each seam. Trim all seam allowances to ¼ in/6 mm, except at the 6 in/15 cm opening. Clip the corners to a 45-degree angle. Turn the quilt Right side out. Use your point turner to push out the corners. Press the seamed edge smooth.

F: Fold under and press the ½ in/12 mm seam allowance at the opening, and pin it. Slipstitch the opening closed by hand. Pin around the circumference of the blanket, and topstitch a ⅜ in/10 mm seam around the outer edge.

G: You have a few choices of how to quilt the blanket. If you wish, you can now "stitch in the ditch" along the pieced seams, machine-topstitching around each square. Or you can use embroidery floss or thread to tack the layers together approximately every 6 in/15 cm along the long seams of the strips.

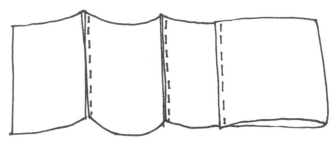

Figure 12

Book Mates/Bookends

These charming peeps are stuffed with batting and some material that will weigh them down (you can use rice or beans, but keep in mind that you cannot wash them then).

This is an easy project and you can whip one of these up in an evening. Use medium-weight cotton for best results. Play around with where you place those ears—it's amazing how different the creatures can look with just that little change.

Finished size:
8 in/20 cm wide x 7½ in/19 cm tall, plus ears

Fabric:
½ yard (44 in wide) /46 cm (114 cm wide) cotton

Supplies:
Pattern from the front pocket of this book
Scissors
Straight pins
Fabric marker
Pencil with eraser
Iron
Thread
1 bag Fiberfil
Piece of paper
Stuffing pellets (or rice, or dry beans)
Hand-sewing needle
Stencil supplies (see page 45)

Notes:
Seams are ½ in/12 mm, except the seam at the bottom of the book mate. The bottom seam is ¼ in/6 mm. The seam allowance is included in the cutting instructions and pattern. Preshrink your fabric by washing, drying, and pressing it before you start.

Step 1: Cut out the pieces from fabric

A: Cut out the pattern pieces provided at the front of this book.

B: Pin the pattern pieces to the Wrong side of the fabric. Align the grain line on the pattern with the grain line of the fabric. Cut 4 pieces for the ears, 2 pieces for the body, and 1 piece for the base following the solid cutting lines on the pattern. Use your fabric marker to mark the placement of the ears on the top of the body pieces, where you want them placed.

Step 2: Sew the book mates

A: With the Right sides of fabric facing each other, pin each set of ears together, leaving the straight side unpinned and open. Carefully stitch around the ears, leaving the opening unstitched, and backstitching at the beginning and end. Trim the seam allowances to ¼ in/6 mm, clip the top point, and clip the curved edges. Turn the ears Right side out through the opening, smoothing the curves with your fingers or the eraser end of a pencil. Press.

B: Place the body pieces Right sides together. Take the ears and sandwich them between the body pieces, aligning the raw edges with the raw edges of the body. Pin around the curved edge of the body, leaving a 2½ in/6 cm opening on the center of one side. Stitch around the body, leaving the opening unstitched, and backstitching at the beginning and end. Trim the seam allowance to ¼ in/6 mm and clip the curve, being careful not to clip though your seam. Do not trim the seam allowance at the opening. [figure 13]

C: With the Right sides together, pin the bottom piece to the body. The narrow curved part of the bottom should align with the side seams of the body. Carefully machine-stitch a ¼ in/6 mm seam, easing in any fullness around the curved bottom and avoiding gathers or puckers, and backstitching at the beginning and end of the seam. Clip around the curved edges, being careful not to clip through your seam.

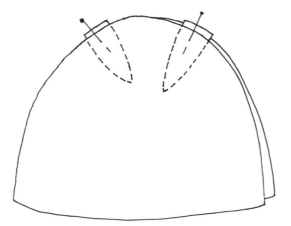

Figure 13

D: Turn the book mate Right side out through the opening. Press around the body and the bottom seam.

E: Stuff the top half of the book mate with the Fiberfil, leaving the bottom 2½ in/6 cm or so unstuffed. Roll the piece of paper into a funnel and insert it into the opening, pointing it toward the bottom of the book mate. Use the funnel to fill the bottom with the stuffing pellets until you've reached a good weight. Fill in any remaining space in the body with a bit more Fiberfil.

F: Fold under ½ in/12 mm on each side of the opening and pin it closed. Slipstitch the opening closed by hand.

G: Stencil the face onto the front of the buddy (see page 44).

Nursing Pillow

There are a bunch of different styles of pillows out there on the market. They can be useful, but are usually unnecessarily expensive, considering that they are so easy to make. These pillows are practical, not only while you are nursing, but also when propping your little newborn up while he lies down (face up, of course), or when he starts, to sit up. I also found that this pillow helped me while I was very pregnant: I laid it between my legs while sleeping on my side. If you want to be able to wash this pillow often, make sure to fill it with polyester batting. You can fill it with wool batting instead, but keep in mind that you will have to undo the seam and empty out all the batting each time you want to wash the cover, which can get too labor-intensive for a new parent.

Finished size:
24 in/61 cm x 19 in/48 cm

Fabric:
1½ yards (44 in wide) /1.4 m (114 cm wide) medium-weight cotton

Supplies:
Pattern from the front pocket of this book
Scissors
Straight pins
Thread
Iron
2 bags Fiberfil or cotton stuffing
Hand-sewing needle

Notes:
All seams are ½ in/12 mm unless otherwise noted. The seam
allowance is included in the cutting instructions and pattern.
Preshrink your fabric by washing, drying, and pressing it
before you start.

Step 1: Cut out the pieces from the fabric

A: Cut out the pattern piece provided at the front of this book.

B: Fold the fabric Right sides together, selvedges aligned. Pin the pattern piece to the fabric, aligning the fold marks with the fold of the fabric and leaving room to cut a second piece. Cut out one layer following the solid cutting lines on the pattern. Re-pin the pattern to the fabric and cut out the second layer.

Step 2: Sew the nursing pillow

A: With the Right sides together, pin the layers together. Keep a 4 in/10 cm opening along the inside straight-ish edge in the curve of the pillow.

B: Machine-stitch around the pillow, making sure to keep the 4 in/10 cm opening unstitched. Trim the seam allowance to ¼ in/6 mm and clip around the curved edges, being careful to not clip through the seam. Do not trim the seam allowance at the opening.

C: Turn the pillow Right side out. Press, smoothing the curved parts with your fingers as you go.

D: Stuff your pillow with the Fiberfil so that it's firm enough to support your child. This could take almost two bags of filling, depending on the firmness you'd like.

E: Press under ½ in/12 mm of the seam allowance at the opening on both sides of the pillow and pin closed. Slipstitch the opening closed by hand.

Towel Hoodie

One of my favorite times with my little August is when we take baths. We often take them together, but he also loves his own little blue tub that is filled to the brim with soapy warm water and rubber dinosaurs. He enjoys his baths a lot and so leaving the warm tub is not a happy moment at all. I made him his own soft towel hoodie, hoping it would make the transition a little less dramatic and much more fuzzy, cuddly, and warm.

This is a quick and easy item to make. You simply sew a bath towel and a hand towel together. I added cotton fabric around the edges to add some personality and style. You can also use a wide ribbon to accent your towel's hoodie.

Finished size:
30 in/76 cm x 30 in/76 cm

Fabric:
1 bath sheet
1 matching hand towel
4 yards (1 in wide) /3.7 m (2.5 cm wide) double-folded bias tape,
or ⅓ yard (44 in wide) /30 cm (114 cm wide) cotton to make your own binding tape

Supplies:
Yardstick
Fabric marker
Scissors
Straight pins
Thread
Iron

Step 1: Cut out the pieces from the fabric

A: Measure and mark the dimensions directly on to the Wrong side of the bath sheet and hand towel, using your yardstick and fabric marker. Cut out each piece following the marked lines.

From the bath sheet: Cut one square: 30 in/76 cm x 30 in/76 cm
From the hand towel: Cut one triangle: 16 in/41 cm x 11 in/28 cm x 11 in/28 cm

Step 2: Make the binding tape (optional)

Tip: because there are no curves, the binding does not need to be cut on the bias.

A: Measure and mark three strips, each 3¾ in/9.5 cm wide x 44 in/112 cm long, on your fabric. Cut out each strip.
B: With the Right sides together, sew the ends of two strips together, trim the seam allowance to ¼ in/6 mm, and press it open. Repeat with the remaining strip.
C: Fold the strip in half lengthwise, Wrong sides together, and press it. Open up the strip and fold each long edge ⅞ in/2.1 cm toward the center fold, pressing as you go. Keeping the edges folded, refold the strip in half along the original center fold.

Step 3: Sew the towel hoodie

A: Begin by enclosing the long edge of the triangle in the binding. Make sure the edge of the toweling is flush with the center fold of the binding, and pin it in place. Carefully machine-stitch close to the edge of the binding, making sure you stitch through all of the layers. Trim the excess binding at each corner of the triangle.

B: Lay the triangle on one corner of the large square, with the bias edge going diagonally across the towel, and both Right sides facing up. Machine-baste the triangle to the square along the two outer edges using a ¼ in/6 mm seam.

C: Enclose the edges of the towel in the binding. Make sure the edge of the toweling is flush with the center fold in the binding. Work your way along the edge of the toweling, pinning as you go.

D: To bind around the corner, fold the bias tape over itself creating a 45-degree mitered corner on both sides. Pin in place.

E: Continue to pin around the other sides, mitering the corners as you go. When you reach the beginning of the binding, fold the end of the bias tape under ½ in/12 mm so that the raw edge is tucked in. Pin it in place.

F: Carefully machine-stitch around all four sides close to the inside edge of the bias tape. Make sure you stitch through all the layers, especially when turning and stitching corners.

Washcloths

You can make a stack of trimmed washcloths and mix and match them. Use the same instructions for the Burp Rags on page 137. You cannot have too many!

Fabric:
1 washcloth
1 yard (½ in wide) /90 cm (12 mm wide) double-folded bias tape

Supplies:
Scissors
Straight pins
Thread

Crib Bumper

I am going to be perfectly honest with you: This was one item I thought we did not need for our little guy. It seemed too lavish and unpractical. But once I placed August in his huge crib, he seemed so tiny and lonely. I quickly changed my mind; I wanted him to feel more padded and secure. A few days later, August had fun patterns surrounding him (and Mommy was much more serene and happy as well).

The bumper will not take you long to make—a couple of evenings perhaps—and you will end up with a unique bumper to cozy up the crib. This project is pretty easy to make. You just have to be calm while wrestling some rather long pieces of material.

Safety note:
The American Academy of Pediatrics cautions that bumpers are a SIDS risk, and they recommend taking them out of the crib before your little one goes to sleep.

Finished size:

The finished bumper will fit a standard 27 in/69 cm x 52 in/132 cm crib. You'll need to adjust the measurements below if your crib is larger or smaller than those dimensions.

Fabric:

4 yards (44 in wide) /3.7 m (114 cm wide) cotton fabric
8 yards (½ in wide) /7.3 m (13 mm wide) trim or ribbon for the ties

Supplies:

Ruler
Fabric marker
Scissors
1 bag (full-sized) extra-loft quilting batting
Hand-sewing needle, long
Thread
Straight pins
Iron

Notes:
All seams are ½ in/12 mm unless otherwise noted. The seam allowance is included in the cutting instructions. Preshrink your fabric by washing, drying, and pressing it before you start.

Step 1: Cut out the pieces from the fabric

A: Fold your fabric in half. Measure and mark the dimensions below directly onto the Wrong side of fabric, using your ruler and fabric marker. Cut out each piece following the marked lines. Measure and mark two rectangles for each size. (Since you're cutting two pieces at once, you'll have four pieces of each size in the end.)

From the fabric:

Cut 4 pieces, with the long side following the fabric's grain: 53½ in/136 cm long x 12 in/30 cm wide

Cut 4 pieces, with the long side following the fabric's grain: 28½ in/72 cm long x 12 in/30 cm wide

From the batting:

Cut 4 pieces: 52 in/132 cm long x 10½ in/27 cm wide

Cut 4 pieces: 27 in/69 cm long x 10½ in/27 cm wide

From the ribbon:

Cut 20 strips: 13 in/33 cm long

114

Step 2: Sew the bumper

A: Make double layers of batting by laying one piece of the larger rectangle on another, and one shorter piece on another. Repeat with other rectangles. You should end up with 2 larger rectangles and 2 smaller rectangles of double layers. Place one large rectangle's short end end-to-end with a smaller rectangle's short end. Use your hand-sewing needle and thread to loosely baste them together. Repeat, alternating the sizes of the rectangles (long, short, long, short). You'll end up with a long strip of batting, and three basted seams.

B: Make two long panels from your cotton. With the Right sides together, pin a large rectangle's short end to a small rectangle's short end. Machine-stitch them together, backstitching at the beginning and end. Repeat using the other two rectangles, alternating sizes (large, small, large, small) until you have a long strip of four rectangles. Repeat with your remaining 4 rectangles. Trim your seam allowances to ¼ in/6 mm and press open.

C: Lay one of your cotton panels fully extended on a flat surface, Wrong side up. Center your batting strip on top of the cotton panel. Using your hand-sewing needle and thread, loosely baste the batting to the fabric 1 in/2.5 cm from the batting's edge. You want to use just enough tension to secure the batting to the fabric without puckering the fabric.

D: On one end of a tie, fold over ¼ in/6 mm, then ¼ in/6 mm again. Press and pin. Repeat on both ends of every tie. Machine-stitch close to the folded-under edge on each tie end, backstitching at the beginning and end. Cut two of the ties in half.

E: Lay the cotton panel without the batting Right side up on a flat surface and measure and mark the placement for the ties using your fabric marker. Fold the ties in half, and align the fold of the tie against the raw edge of the fabric with the tie ends pointing inward. On both the top and the bottom of the panel place one on each seam, one in the center of the short panels, and two centered in the long panel. Pin them in place. Pin one halved tie at the top of one end corner, and one at the bottom. You can check the tie placement against your crib if you wish and adjust them so that the ties match up with the slats. Machine-baste the ties to the fabric using a ¼ in/6 mm seam. You'll have one halved tie left over; that's okay. [figure 14]

F: With the Right sides of the cotton fabrics facing each other, the batting on the outside, and the ties sandwiched between the two layers, pin the two fabric panels together leaving the end without the ties open. Machine-stitch along all three sides. Be sure to sew the ties in the seam, but do not catch the loose ends, and backstitch at the beginning and end. Trim the seam allowance to ¼ in/6 mm, but do not trim the seam allowance at the opening. Clip the corners to a 45-degree angle. Turn the bumper Right side out through the opening, and smooth out the corners. Press.

G: Fold ½ in/12 mm under on both sides of the open end, and press. Insert the remaining tie halves at top of each corner and pin in place. Pin the opening closed. Hand-sew the opening closed, securing the ties as you sew.

H: Topstitch ½ in/12 mm from the seamed edge around the entire bumper. Press down on the batting to ease the bumper through your machine, securing the batting in the seam, and backstitching at the beginning and end.

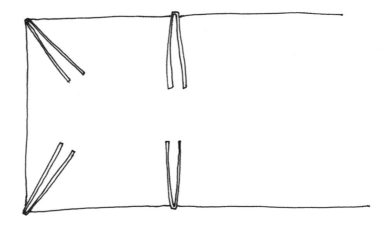

Figure 14

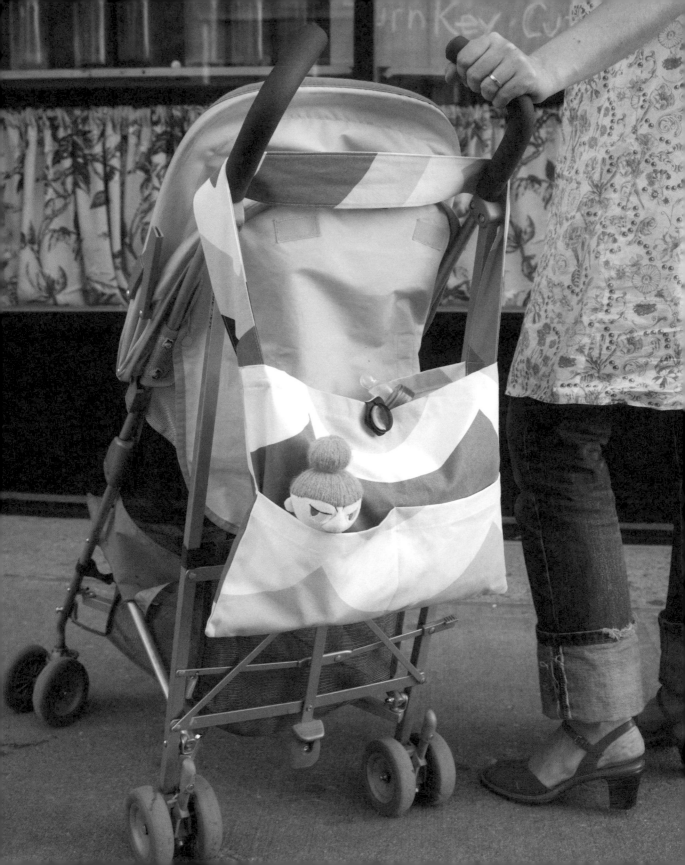

Diaper Bag

I decided to make a simple bag for my stroller. It's nothing fancy—just a bag that will hold the most-needed items for an outing. The straps are long and it's styled sort of like a messenger bag, so it will not only fit around most strollers, but it will also fit around most people. There are two front pockets where the mobile phone and the binkie will be easily accessible at all times. I recommend a sturdy fabric, such as canvas, for this project. While you are at it, why not personalize it with some swift stencil work of your own (see page 44)?

Finished size:
16½ in/42 cm wide x 12 in/30 cm tall, with a 31 in/79 cm-long strap

Fabric:
1 yard (44 in wide) /90 cm (114 cm wide) medium to heavy cotton, twill, or canvas
7 in (½ in wide) /18 cm (12 mm wide) ribbon or trim

Supplies:
Ruler
Fabric marker
Scissors
Iron
Thread
Fadeout marker
Straight pins
Hand-sewing needle
Point turner
Pinking shears (optional)
Button

Notes:
All seams are ½ in/12 mm unless otherwise noted. The seam allowance is included in the cutting instructions. Preshrink your fabric by washing, drying, and pressing it before you start.

Step 1: Cut out the pieces from the fabric

A: Measure and mark the dimensions below directly onto the Wrong side of fabric, using your ruler and fabric marker. Cut out each piece following the marked lines.

For the pocket, cut 1 piece: 17 in/43 cm wide x 8½ in/22 cm long

For the bag's body, cut 2 pieces: 17 in/43 cm wide x 13½ in/34 cm long

For the strap, cut 1 piece with the long side on the fold: 3 in/8 cm wide x 34 in/86 cm long (unfolded size: 6 in/15 cm x 34 in/86 cm)

Step 2: Make the pocket and strap

A: With the pocket's Wrong side facing you, fold over ½ in/12 mm along the long side and press. Fold over 1 in/2.5 cm again and press. Machine-stitch a seam along the folded-under edge, backstitching at the beginning and end. On the Right side of the fabric, measure halfway down the long side and mark it with your fadeout marker. Measure halfway down the other long side and mark it. Using your ruler, draw a line between the two marks.

B: With the Right side of one body panel facing you, lay the pocket panel Right side up on top of the body panel, aligning the pocket's raw long edge with one raw long edge of the body panel. Pin the two pieces together along the fadeout marker line you just made. Machine-stitch along the marked line, making sure to backstitch at the beginning and end of the seam. [figure 15]

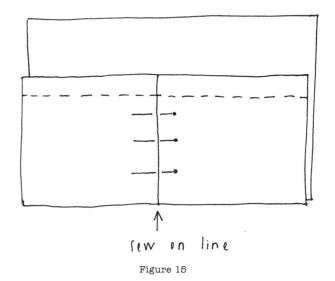

sew on line

Figure 15

C: With the strap's Wrong side facing up, fold it in half lengthwise, then press a crease on the fold. Open the piece so that the Wrong side faces up. Fold the two long sides ½ in/12 mm toward the crease. Press, then fold it in half lengthwise, Right side out. Match up the long folded edges (opposite the crease), and topstitch them together, using a ⅛ in/3 mm seam, backstitching at each end. Make sure you stitch through all the layers. Press under ½ in/12 mm on each raw end of the strap.

Step 3: Make the diaper bag

A: With the Right sides of the body pieces facing each other, pin along the short sides and the long edge that the pocket is aligned with. Machine-stitch along these three sides. Clip the two corners to a 45-degree angle. Zigzag the seam allowance (or use your pinking shears to trim it to ¼ in/6 mm). Turn the bag Right side out, and use your point turner to square the corners. Press the seams.

B: Turn the bag Wrong side out. Fold over ½ in/12 mm along the top raw edge and press. Fold over 1 in/2.5 cm again and press and pin.

C: Fold the ribbon in half so that the ends lie side by side: It will be U-shaped. Find the center top of the bag's non-pocket side and make a small mark on the inside with your fadeout marker. Insert both the folded raw ends under the folded-over hem at the center mark. Fold the button loop up so it sticks out over the top of the bag. Pin it in place. Machine-stitch a seam close to the folded-under edge around the bag's top, backstitching at the beginning and end. Machine-stitch a rectangle around the part of the ribbon that overlaps the hem to secure it. [figure 16]

D: Place the shoulder strap's folded-under ½ in/12 mm raw ends just below the top hem at the side seams of the bag (one strap end at each side seam), being careful not to twist the strap. Pin it in place. Machine-stitch a rectangle around the bottom of the straps through all the layers including the top hem, as shown, being sure to backstitch at the beginning and end.

E: Find the center top of the pocket side of the bag and make a small mark on the outside, about 1 in/2.5 cm from the top. Using your hand-sewing needle and thread, securely sew the button where you've made the mark.

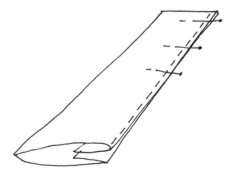

Figure 16

Changing Pad

This will to be one of the items you'll use the most while out and about with your baby. I live a pretty active life—outings to restaurants, trips to Japan, evenings at galleries, errands to the post office, visits to the Finnish consulate— and my son, August, always comes along, so a changing pad is crucial. This one is slightly padded for comfort, but rolls up easily and won't be too bulky in your bag. Use polyester padding so you can wash this pad over and over. Once you have one of these, you can get out there and explore the world with your little one!

Finished size:

28 in/71 cm long x 19 in/48 cm wide

Fabric:

¾ yard (44 in wide) /70 cm (114 cm wide) lightweight cotton for the inside of the pad

¾ yard (44 in wide) /70 cm (114 cm wide) medium to heavy cotton, twill, or canvas for the outside of the pad

Very thin quilting batting

13½ in (1 in wide) /34 cm (2.5 cm wide) grosgrain ribbon or twill tape

Supplies:

Ruler

Fabric marker

Scissors

Fadeout marker

Straight pins

Thread

3 in (1 in wide) /8 cm (2.5 cm wide) Velcro

Iron

Point turner

Notes:

All seams are ½ in/12 mm unless otherwise noted. The seam allowance is included in the cutting instructions. Preshrink your fabric by washing, drying, and pressing it before you start.

Step 1: Cut out the pieces from the fabric

A: Measure and mark the dimensions below directly on to the Wrong side of fabric, using your ruler and fabric marker. Cut out each piece following the marked lines.

From the lightweight cotton: Cut 1 piece: 29 in/74 cm long x 20 in/51 cm wide

From the heavier fabric: Cut 1 piece: 29 in/74 cm long x 20 in/51 cm wide

From the batting: Cut 1 piece: 29 in/74 cm long x 20 in/51 cm wide

Step 2: Make the changing pad

A: Using your ruler and fadeout marker, mark the lines to quilt the batting to the lightweight cotton layer. On the Right side, start ½ in/12 mm in from one end of the fabric's long side, and make a mark every 3½ in/9 cm. Repeat along the other long edge. Join the marks so you have lines drawn across the entire piece.

B: Pin your batting flat against the Wrong side of the lightweight cotton. Machine-baste them together using a ¼ in/6 mm seam around the entire piece. Turn the piece so the Right side is facing you, and machine-stitch along the quilting lines you drew, securing the batting to the cotton, and backstitching at the beginning and end.

C: Pull the Velcro apart, and place one side of the Velcro ½ in/12 mm from the ribbon's end. Pin to secure. Machine-stitch the Velcro to the ribbon along the very edge of the Velcro around all four sides.

D: Flip the ribbon over. On the opposite end from the one you just stitched the Velcro to, fold up the end of the ribbon ½ in/12 mm and press. With the folded part facing you, place the other piece of Velcro on top of the folded part ¼ in/6 mm from the fold. Pin to secure and machine-stitch the Velcro to the ribbon along the very edge of the Velcro around all four sides. You should now have a piece of Velcro on each side, and each end, of the ribbon.

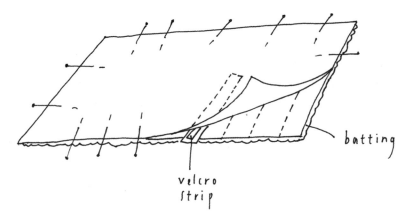

velcro
strip

batting

Figure 17

E: With the fabrics' Right sides facing each other and the batting on the outside, pin the two fabric pieces together leaving a 6 in/15 cm opening along one long edge. Measure 14½ in/37 cm down one long side of the fabric and sandwich the ribbon with the Velcro between the Right sides of the fabric. The ribbon's raw edge should align with the fabric's raw edge, and the Velcro tab near the raw edge should face away from the batting layer. Machine-stitch along all sides, making sure to leave the 6 in/15 cm opening along one side. Trim the seam allowance to ¼ in/6 mm, but do not trim the seam allowance at the opening. Clip the corners to a 45-degree angle. Turn the pad Right side out through the opening, using your point turner to poke out the corners. Press. [figure 17]

F: Fold under, pin, and press the ½ in/12 mm seam allowance at the opening. Topstitch ¼ in/6 mm from the seamed edge around the entire blanket, securing the open seam allowance in the topstitching.

Step 3: Roll up the changing pad

A: With the quilted part facing you and the ribbon on top, fold the right and left sides toward the center. Starting at the side opposite the ribbon, roll the pad toward the ribbon. Finally, wrap the ribbon around the blanket and Velcro it closed.

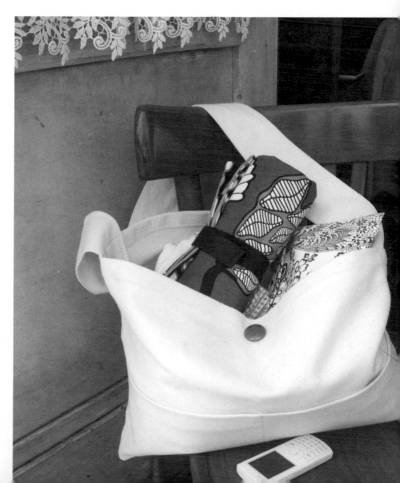

Velcro Pouches

These bags—so much more stylish than zipper-top plastic baggies—will come in handy all the time. I use them to store nappies, rags, binkies, snacks, and backup creepers, to name just a few of the things my son, August, and I take with us when we're running errands.

These pouches are easy to make. There are no zippers to sew (Velcro is so much more user-friendly for a multitasking mom with her hands full). You can make these pouches in all kinds of sizes—it's up to you and your needs. Why not sew a few pouches out of oilcloth fabric as well as a few regular cotton ones?

Finished size:
The small pouch is 6 in/15 cm long x 7 in/18 cm wide; the large pouch is 9½ in/24 cm long x 10 in/25 cm wide

Fabric:
⅓ yard (44 in wide) /30 cm (114 cm wide) lightweight cotton for the small pouch
⅓ yard (44 in wide) /30 cm (114 cm wide) heavier weight cotton for the large pouch

Notes:
All seams are ½ in/12 mm unless otherwise noted. The seam allowance is included in the cutting instructions. Preshrink your fabric by washing, drying, and pressing it before you start.

Supplies:
Ruler
Fabric marker
Scissors
Iron
Fadeout marker
12 in (½ in wide) /30 cm (12 mm wide) Velcro
Straight pins
Point turner

Step 1: Cut out the pieces from the fabric

A: Measure and mark the dimensions directly onto the Wrong side of fabric, using your ruler and fabric marker. Cut out each piece following the marked lines.

From the fabric:
For the small pouch, cut 1 piece: 8 in/20 cm wide x 18 in/46 cm long
For the large pouch, cut 1 piece: 11 in/28 cm wide x 24 in/61 cm long

From the Velcro:
For the small pouch, cut 1 piece: 5½ in/14 cm long
For the large pouch, cut 1 piece: 8½ in/22 cm long

Step 2: Sew the pouches

A: On both the small and large pouch pieces, with the Wrong side facing you, fold over ¼ in/6 mm along one short side and press. Fold over another ¼ in/6 mm and press again. Machine-stitch close to the folded-under edge.

B: On the small pouch, with the Right side facing you, measure down 2⅛ in/5.4 cm from the top of the stitched seam and use your fadeout marker to draw a line across the pouch. Repeat for the large pouch, but measure down 3¼ in/8.3 cm. Take the fluffy side of the shorter Velcro piece and place it so the top edge is aligned with your mark, and the piece is centered on the pouch from side to side. Repeat for the large pouch using the fluffy side of the larger Velcro piece. Machine-stitch around each side of the Velcro, backstitching at the beginning and end.

C: On the small pouch's other short end, with the Wrong side facing you, fold over ½ in/12 mm and press, then fold over 1 in/2.5 cm and press again. Repeat on the large pouch. On the small pouch, with the Right side facing you, unfold the hem you just pressed. Take the rough side of the shorter Velcro piece and center it in the middle, and side to side, of the 1 in/2.5 cm pressed area. Machine-stitch around each side of the Velcro, backstitching at the beginning and end. Repeat for the large pouch using the rough side of the larger Velcro piece. With the Wrong side facing you, fold over the pressed hem you just sewed the Velcro on and machine-stitch across the hem close to the folded-under edge. Repeat for the large pouch. [figure 18]

D: With the small pouch's Right side facing you and the 1 in/2.5 cm hemmed seam at the top, fold up 6 in/15 cm of the bottom toward the pouch's top. Pin and machine-stitch a seam from the fold to the top of the ¼ in/6 mm hemmed edge on both sides of the pouch. Trim the seam allowances to ¼ in/6 mm, clip the bottom corners to 45 degrees, and zigzag along the edge of the seam allowance to prevent fraying. Turn the pouch Right side out and use your point turner to smooth the corner. Press. Repeat for the large pouch, only fold up 9 in/23 cm instead.

E: Place the small pouch open in front of you. Fold the top flap's outer edges in by ¼ in/6 mm and press. Then fold in another ¼ in/6 mm and press. Machine-stitch close to the folded-under edge between the top of the flap and the opening of the pouch. Repeat for the large pouch.

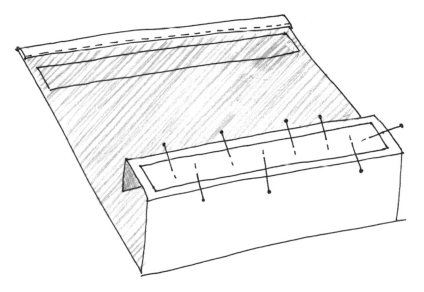

Figure 18

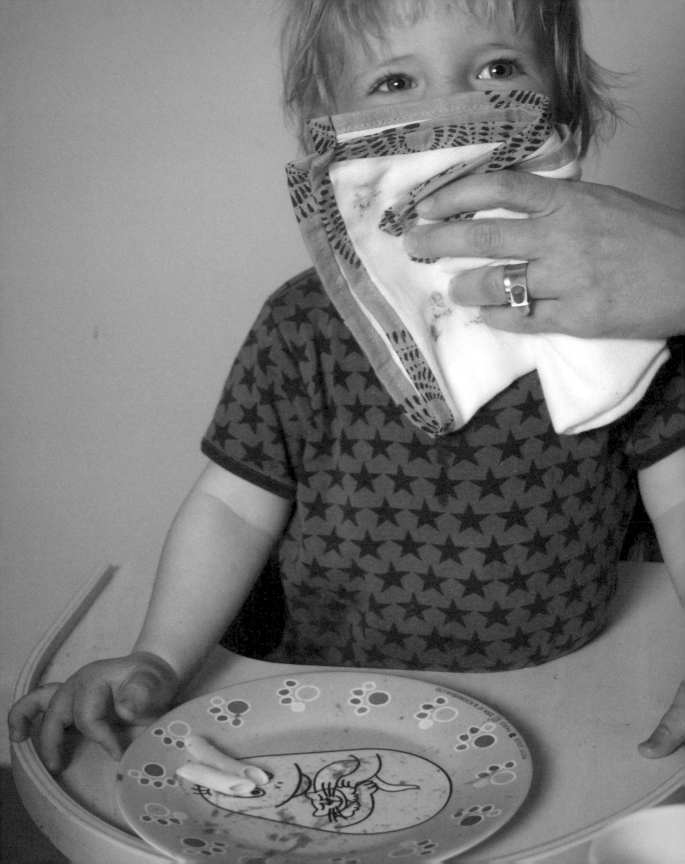

Burp Rags

Oh dear, I had no idea! Babies drool and spit up—a lot—and all the time! You constantly have to be ready to mop. I cannot tell you how many rags I would go through each day when my little August was brand new. I still have a stack of rags at hand, and I always make sure to pack at least one when we go out. I bought a bunch of cloth diapers for this purpose; they wash well and are economical. To spiff them up and to make this wiping process a wee bit more fun, I added some decorative edging. I recommend making a stack of at least ten of them.

Fabric:

1 cotton diaper
2 yards (½ in wide) /1.8 m (12 mm wide) double-folded bias tape

Supplies:

Scissors
Straight pins
Thread

Step 1: Attach the bias tape

A: Enclose the edges of the diaper in the bias tape. Make sure that the diaper's edge is flush with the center fold in the bias tape. Work your way along the edge of the diaper, pinning as you go.

B: To bind around the corner, fold the bias tape over itself creating a 45-degree mitered corner on both sides. Pin in place. [figure 19]

C: Continue to pin around the other sides, mitering the corners as you go. When you reach the corner where you started, fold the end of the bias tape under ½ in/12 mm so that the raw edge is tucked in. Pin in place.

D: Carefully machine-stitch around all four sides, sewing close to the inside edge of the bias tape. Make sure you stitch through all the layers, especially when turning and stitching corners.

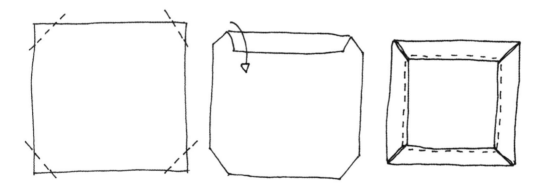

Figure 19

Resources:

Lotta Jansdotter

If you find yourself in Brooklyn, please stop by our studio shop for a visit (but make an appointment first!). We have a small run of fabrics, scrap bags, and notions. Find out more at:
www.jansdotter.com

Retail Stores:

San Francisco

Britex Fabrics

If you visit San Francisco, make sure that you go to Britex Fabrics. It's a landmark destination for anybody who loves fabrics and notions.

146 Geary Street
San Francisco, CA 94108
(415) 392-2910
www.britexfabrics.com

Craft Gym

Craft Gym offers workshops and open studio time in sewing, knitting, ceramics, metals, paper, wood, and textiles.

1452 Bush Street
San Francisco, CA 94109
(415) 702-5700
www.craftgym.com

Portland, Oregon

Bolt Fabric Boutique

A great fabric shop that also offers sewing classes.

2136 NE Alberta Street
Portland, OR 97211
(503) 287-2658
www.boltfabricboutique.com

New York

If you find yourself in Manhattan, get ready to shop for some fabrics! There's a whole slew of fabric shops in the Garment District. I have listed a few of my favorites here:

M&J Trimming

You can spend a great amount of time in this store. M&J Trimming stocks almost everything you might need in trims: ribbons, elastic tape, buttons, and tassels—it never ends! They have an amazing array of choices. It is simply the best resource for trims. If you cannot visit their store, they also have a Web site where you can shop.

1008 Sixth Avenue
New York, NY 10018
(800) 965-8746
www.mjtrim.com

B&J Fabrics

This is a family-owned fabric store with a remarkable selection of beautiful fabrics—their inventory will make you swoon. If you're into sewing it's the place to shop, with a wonderful and knowledgeable staff.

525 7th Avenue
New York, NY 10018
(212) 354-8150
www.bandjfabrics.com

Mood Designer Fabrics

Yes, it's true—it really is amazing. Not only do they have an endless amount of fabrics and so many, many different choices, their staff is also very friendly and helpful. This is simply a "must visit" while in New York. Last time I spent four hours there—honest truth.

225 W 37th Street, Third Floor
New York, NY 10018
(212) 730-5003
www.moodfabrics.com

There is also a Mood location in Los Angeles—yay!

6151 W. Pico Blvd.
Los Angeles, CA 90035
(323) 653-6663
www.moodfabrics.com

Brooklyn General Store

This welcoming and warm shop carries fabrics, yarns, and great sewing books. They also offer classes. It is located just around the corner from my apartment—lucky me!

128 Union Street
Brooklyn, NY 11231
(718) 237-7753
www.brooklyngeneral.com

Purl Patchwork

A more organized and well-selected little fabric shop will be very hard to find. It's a gem! Visit this little, but yet mighty, shop located in New York or, second best, their Web site:

147 Sullivan Street
New York, NY 10012
(212) 420-8798
www.purlsoho.com

Make Workshop

Sewing classes (and a lot of other great craft classes) in Manhattan:

195 Chrystie Street, #402F
New York, NY 10002
(212) 533-9995
www.makeworkshop.com

Online Resources:

Virginia Johnson, a friend of mine, designs the most amazing cotton fabrics. Her designs are so sunny, happy, vibrant, and colorful, they make me smile and feel good. Find her fabrics (and also some rather nice clothing and totes) online at:

www.virginiajohnson.com

Denyse Schmidt is an incredibly talented designer and quilter with a modern take on an old technique. She also designs fabrics. Find fabric and scrap bags on her Web site:

www.dsquilts.com

Amy Butler designs colorful and inspiring fabrics. Visit her Web site and search under "where to buy" to find retailers that carry her fabrics:

www.amybutlerdesign.com

Designer **Paula Smail** is inspired by her travels, apricot trees, and Japanese gardens. You can buy fabric scrap bags on her Web site, perfect for smaller projects or quilts:

www.henryroad.com

Sweet florals and pretty patterns by **Anna Maria Horner**:
www.annamariahorner.com

I grew up with **Marimekko** fabrics all around me, thanks to my mother who used their material in our home and for herself. I've used Marimekko fabrics for many of the projects in this book. Luckily for all of us, their fabrics are available online:
www.kiitosmarimekko.com

Modern, retro-inspired, and simply great fabrics created by a husband and wife team in Brooklyn:
www.twenty2.net

Vintage-inspired patterns on barkcloth, hand-printed in San Francisco:
www.melinamade.com

Reprodepot Fabrics has the best selection of reproduction fabrics. The prints are so fun and inspiring, and are sold at very good prices. This company is owned and run by one really nice lady:
www.reprodepotfabrics.com

A user-friendly site, with notions and a wide selection of fabrics:
www.sewmamasew.com

To find a nice selection of hemp fabrics, visit:
www.hemptraders.com

Fabrics made out of bamboo:
www.bamboofabricstore.com

I have to admit: I love IKEA! They carry a limited, but very nice, collection of fabrics by the yard at incredibly low prices. They don't sell fabric online, but go to their Web site to find a store near you:
www.ikea.com

T-shirt blanks to print on:
www.americanapparel.net
www.alternativeapparel.com
www.article1.net

Art and craft supplies:
www.michaels.com
www.pearlpaint.com
www.joann.com

Index: